A KITCHEN SURVIVAL COOKBOOK

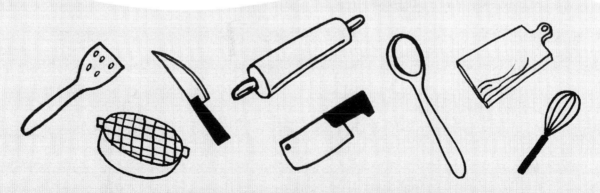

Chef Gordon Smith and Reparata Mazzola

Copyright © 2013 Gordon Smith and Reparata Mazzola

Save The Males Publishing
www.savethemales.com

All rights reserved. No part of this publication may be reproduced, stored in a retrieval system, or transmitted in any form or by any means, electronic, mechanical, photocopying, recording, or otherwise, without permission of the authors.

ISBN 13: 978-0-615-89983-1
ISBN 10:   0-615-89983-8
Library of Congress No. Pending

Printed and bound in the USA by Chromatic, Inc., Los Angeles, CA
Founders of Green Print Alliance.
Renewable resources were used to print this book.

Cover design and illustrations © Lindy Bostrom 2013/BostromGraphics.com

Notice: This book presents information gleaned from personal experiences along with research. The author and publisher are not offering or dispensing medical advice for any health-related issues.

Man is a Cooking Animal...

"Gentlemen," said Mr. Perrigine Touchwood, "Man is a cooking animal and in whatever situation he is found, it may be assumed, as an axiom, that his progress in civilization has kept exact pace with the degree of refinement he may have attained in the art of gastronomy—from the hairy man in the woods...to the modern gourmet."

The Cooks and the Housewife's Manual (introduction)
— Margaret Dods (1826)

Dedication

This book is dedicated to my Mom, Reba Smith. We had fun together watching Julia Child's cooking show and *The Galloping Gourmet*. Born and raised in Savannah, Georgia, she made the best Southern comfort food for our family. All of her dishes were infused with one unwritten ingredient...love.

Thanks to:

Lindy Bostrom our amazing book designer and illustrator. Cyrene Houdini for her video magic. Chef Peter Hall, my mentor and friend who started me on my culinary path. Greg Koch for his unique input. Special thanks to my family and friends who have listened to me talk about the Save The Males for years.

Extra special thanks to my partner Reparata who made my dream a beautifully written reality.

And nothing I have done in my life would have been possible without the support of my father, Al, my son Kalani, and my brothers, my twin Greg, and Matthew.

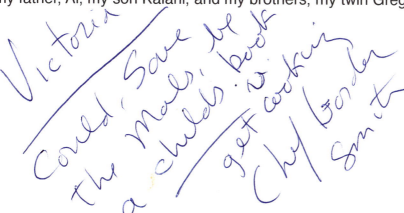

INTRODUCTION

Save the Males is not one of those macho cookbooks that teach you how to grill the critters you kill or make meals with your garage tools. It's a kitchen compass to help you navigate culinary waters and much more. It will help you take charge of your food reality and when you learn to be self-sufficient, you'll see that cooking is not only good for you, it can improve your health, your appearance and even your sex life.

In *Save the Males*, I'm giving you the benefit of what I've learned. The idea came to me when I was suddenly single, thrust out into the world after a bitter divorce. I went back to college and roomed with two guys who didn't know how to boil water; I didn't know much more. Left to our own culinary devices, the three of us ate fast-food, take-out or frozen dinners. My health went downhill from the stress of not being able to see my two-year-old son, a heavy class schedule and bad eating habits. Plus, I was putting myself through school and needed a job. I had to save myself. Peter Hall, the chef/owner of an upscale seafood restaurant in Sacramento, hired me as a grunt prep cook. I cleaned what seemed like endless pounds of shrimp, cut up cases of broccoli, made gallons of salad dressing and did whatever else needed to be done. All the while, I watched Peter create exquisitely prepared dishes. What struck me was that he really enjoyed his work. I wanted to learn more. He took me under his wing; my basic training began. I worked my way up to become his sous chef and eventually helped Peter open a new restaurant. I learned my trade from the ground up. I was fortunate to have been schooled by, and work with, some of the greatest master chefs in the business. I became good enough to be a member of the U.S. Culinary Olympic Team that was awarded a silver medal. As assistant production manager for the Los Angeles Olympics, I helped cater three meals a day for 7,000 athletes.

I've owned my own restaurant, fed over 10,000 guests a week at the Squaw Valley Ski Resort and learned spa cuisine from the incomparable Michel Stroot of the Golden Door. That led to a job as head chef at Cal-A-Vie Spa. There I helped train a young Rosie Daley, who went on to work for Oprah Winfrey and wrote the best seller, In the Kitchen with Rosie. As a private chef, I consulted for Deepak Chopra's Center for Well Being, cooked for royalty, celebrities and families. I had my share of food fiascoes in those early days but gradually found that not only was cooking relaxing, I was healthier and more optimistic. That's when I decided that someday I would share my experiences with other men who find themselves on their own.

The 21st Century male needs help even more now than I did years ago. Men today are under tremendous stress. We're burdened by work, zoned out by competition, expected to be creative, make money and hurdle insurmountable problems with the aplomb of James Bond, while women want us to be strong, sensitive, affectionate, passionate, playful, intuitive, communicative and complimentary. We're still feeling the fallout from the days when radical feminists turned women with flowers in their hair into man-eating plants. The battle of the sexes escalated into a war. Men were declared the enemy. "I can do it" all but eliminated our primitive male urge to protect the female—we couldn't even open a door for a date.

Is it any wonder that men settle into a sofa at day's end, soothed by the remote control or rush off to golf courses driving Titleists in one direction or go whacky at mid-life? Don't reach for a bimbo, a bottle or a bunch of junk food—consider cooking. It's a damned good way to restore your sanity and feed your soul. The kitchen is a place where you can feel successful because you've completed a project from start to finish. I look forward to sharing my tips and shortcuts with you. Empower yourself. Get cooking and get healthy. *Save the Males* is not just a kitchen survival cookbook —it's a whole new way of life.

Chef Gordon Smith

x Save The Males Cookbook

A Note from Reparata

When I got the opportunity to collaborate on *Save the Males* I was hesitant. Like many women I had to ask, "Why do males need saving?" They're not a downtrodden minority. They run the majority of Fortune 500 companies, get paid more and don't have to go through childbirth. Then I met Chef Gordon Smith. He was founder of the San Diego chapter of Slow Food, a movement to preserve cultural food traditions. That interested me. I grew up in Brooklyn and learned to cook amazing Italian dishes from my Mom. Gordon told me about *Save the Males*, his mission to help men who are clueless in the kitchen. He was also passionate about giving men a healthy alternative to the drive thru and wanted to show them how cooking was a way to alleviate stress. Men need ways to relax today more than ever in this multi-tasking, social media world. To compound that, for a variety of reasons, some men find themselves suddenly home alone in the kitchen. It can be scary but it's just a room. *Save the Males* can demystify it. This book is a roadmap to get you from an empty kitchen to a place where you can actually cook a meal for friends and loved ones.

Save the Males makes men less dependent on women for food. It's a good thing. It doesn't mean they can do without us or we can do without them. It's about lightening up. It's about caring. This book is not meant to be sexist…I hope women will enjoy the humor.

So, whether you're a man on your own, or a home cook who can use a refresher course, or a woman who knows some poor malnourished single guy, this book is for you. I want to keep my men healthy…**I want to *Save the Males* for me!** This collaboration has been one of the most rewarding writing ventures I have experienced. If we can get even one man on a fast track to cooking for himself, then we've done something.

Enjoy the book!

Reparata Mazzola

TABLE OF CONTENTS

1 YOUR EQUIPMENT DOES MATTER 15
Essential Kitchen Utensils
Fearless Grocery Shopping
Stocking Your Pantry
Food Storage Guides
How to Read a Recipe
Basic Cooking Techniques

2 COOK FOR A DAY—EAT FOR A WEEK 41
What to Freeze, How to Thaw and Other Kitchen Science
Foolproof Cooking Techniques for Rice, Pasta Meat and Potatoes
Pasta Sauces to Serve And Save
The Incredible Edible Potato
Cuts of Beef
Mouthwatering Meatloaf

3 RECIPES FOR ROMANCE. 77
My Culinary Creed for Romance
Facts About Aphrodisiacs
Matching Menus to Your Date's Personality
Matching Food to Your Date's Zodiac sign
How Set a Table
Erotic Appetizers, Enticing Entrees, Delectable Desserts
Amorous Breakfasts

4 EAT WELL—WEIGH LESS. 103
Why it's Hard to Lose Weight
How Food Changes Your Metabolism
The Truth About Carbs, Gluten-Free and Cholesterol
Fat Facts and Fiction
Deciphering Nutrition Labels
Personal Tips to Drop Pounds and Keep Them Off
Recipes That Won't Feel Like Diet Food

5 PARTY HEALTHY 133
Good-Time, Guilt-Free Recipes
What to Eat at a Party That Won't Kill You
Tips for Take Out
The Booze You Choose
Hangover Causes and Cures

6 HELP! I'M HOME ALONE WITH THE KIDS! 153
Keeping Kids Safe in the Kitchen
Fun Recipes to Cook Together (that they'll like)
Simple Pancake Shapes
No Cook Desserts
Easy Instructions to Make a Bunny Cake (really)

7 RESCUE REMEDIES. 173
What to Do When Things Go Wrong
Emergency Basics
Things Your Father Never Told You
Other Good Stuff to Know

8 OTHER FOOD FOR THOUGHT 187
Grow Your Own - Know Where Your Food Comes From
Vertical Growing- Create a Garden With Limited Space
How to Tell What's Really Organic
What to Know About GMO
Demystifying Sweeteners
Food Matters: Why "Superfoods" are Super

About the Authors 203

Webliography 205

Appendix 211

Index 223

CHAPTER 1

YOUR EQUIPMENT DOES MATTER

A kitchen is just a room. It's nothing to be afraid of. Consider cooking like you do sports—you can't win without the right gear. I've had men ask me why they need to have any more equipment than a frying pan and a can opener. It's simple. Your kitchen is like your toolbox. You wouldn't use a flat head screwdriver on a Phillips screw. A jig saw is not a chain saw. Pliers are not a ratchet wrench. Each tool has a specific job. That's true for knives, pots, pans and utensils. Would you carve a turkey with a paring knife or fry an egg in a spaghetti pot? You can peel potatoes with a utility knife but once you see the efficiency of a real peeler, you'll know why you'll want one. If you like gadgets, once you get into cooking you'll want to have them all, from cherry pitters to a tool that makes hard-boiled egg cubes. You don't need a huge capital investment to have a well-equipped kitchen. There are reasonably priced items in every category I'm going to mention. You can buy them at a kitchen store or find them at swap meets and garage sales. The tools in this chapter are the essentials to get you started. You can buy them all at once or slowly build your culinary arsenal.

FIRST THINGS FIRST—KNIVES

Assuming you are starting from scratch, the first thing you need are a few good knives. Questions I get most often are: "Which ones should I buy?" and "Which one should I use?" First, this is the one item you shouldn't scrimp on. Good knives, properly cared for, can last a lifetime and are a chef's most valued professional possession. Get the best you can afford and I don't mean a whole set for twenty bucks. The best blades are high-carbon stainless steel. Ceramic knives are the latest craze, but there are disadvantages. They aren't as hard as steel and could shatter or chip. A lot of elite-level chefs are switching from the heavier blades to thinner Japanese knives with lighter edges. They need less sharpening but are very pricey and without proper use, are also susceptible to chipping.

You can buy knives on the Internet or from a home shopping channel on TV, but my advice is to go to a kitchen store for a hands-on tryout. Hold the knife to see if it's a good fit. Different manufacturers have different contours. How comfortable is the grip? It should feel like an extension of your hand. Look for sturdy construction that will endure lots of wear and tear. A quality blade extends into the handle (the "tang") and is held in place by rivets. Cheap knives are glued and loosen in washing; you'll have to replace them every few years. Modern chefs are using stainless steel handles forged into the blade.

Sharpening steel

Sharpening stone

Each time you use a knife, a microscopic portion of the blade is bent. Keep the blades sharp with a good sharpening stone and a 10" sharpening steel. Pull your knife lightly across the steel at a 20 degree angle, covering the entire blade and alternating sides. Do the same with a stone. When your knife no longer feels sharp after "steeling" or "stoning," take it to a professional sharpener. Some can openers have a grinder feature but they can get very hot and ruin the blade. If you want to go electric, invest in a sharpener. Never scrape food from a cutting board with the blade—this makes it dull—always use the back of the knife to pick up food. Don't use a knife to pry off jar covers, cut twine, open cardboard boxes, clean your fingernails or do anything else with them but prepare food. You can store knives in a wooden block or get one of those magnetic holders mounted on the wall. Either method will keep them out of the reach of young children. Don't throw knives in a kitchen drawer on top of one another. This can destroy the blades. Don't throw your knives into the sink because it can nick them. Although knives won't be destroyed by cleaning them in the dishwasher, it's not a good practice. They can get damaged by rattling around with other silverware; plastic handles may get discolored by detergents and wooden ones are damaged by soaking. Wash them when you're finished and put them away.

So, how many knives do you need to start? You'll need four basic ones. I've prepared some of my best meals using just one cleaver but that may be awkward for a novice. Your most essential tool is a chef's knife. This is the workhorse of the kitchen and the most versatile. Its blade tapers to the tip and is used in a rocking motion for chopping or slicing. The wide part allows the cook's hand to guide the movement. Chef's knives can be used to prepare most anything from cutting veggies to slicing meat.

I recommend two chef's knives initially: a 6" and an 8" blade. A 10" blade can be hard to handle for beginners but the longer the blade, the easier it is to control. A small paring knife is the third knife you'll need. Use this one for peeling and coring fruits and vegetable or slicing small objects. The blade is 3" to 4" long and is easy to control.

Rivets

8" Serrated knife

A serrated knife has a jagged blade and is great for slicing everything from thick crusted breads to tomatoes. I recommend one 8" in length. Use this knife with an even-pressured sawing motion. Don't squash what you're cutting by holding the item too tight. One great feature of a serrated blade is that it doesn't need sharpening.

POTS AND PANS YOU CAN'T LIVE WITHOUT

Next, we come to an equally important item in equipping the kitchen: pots and pans. When you go into a store you'll see shelves stacked with different styles, finishes and sizes. Your grandmother cooked with cast iron and chefs love it; I think it's too heavy and unwieldy for a new cook. Copper is the best heat conductor but it's expensive. Aluminum is the next best choice but certain foods can react with the metal giving them a tinny taste. Some research has even linked aluminum to Alzheimer's[1]. I remember my Mom's old metal coffee pot and pans. Today, aluminum is safer because the fused coating stops the metal from leeching into the food. Stainless steel is excellent but doesn't conduct heat well unless it has a copper bottom. A good compromise is a stainless pot with a thin copper strip around it.

There are good quality, nonstick surfaces like Teflon™ or Silverstone™ that are easy to use and make clean up a breeze. When you cook in nonstick pots and pans, only use wooden or coated utensils because metal scratches the coating and it gets into your food. Some companies advertise "scratch proof" but I still would not use metal on it. Never put nonstick cookware into the dishwasher.

GORDON SAYS: *Some say nonstick coating releases toxic fumes when it overheats causing "Teflon Fever" with flu-like symptoms, but if there is food in the pan it can't overheat, since the food cools it down. Just be careful preheating any nonstick pan, otherwise it's safe to cook with.*

---

1. *Journal of Alzheimer's Disease* online, Vol. 35, No. 1

You can get cookware online or from those TV offers but you can't really see the quality and flimsy pots are a waste of money. You don't need to buy a whole set right away, just get ones you need. Once again, go into a store and try them out. Look at the handles. They should be firmly connected, riveted or screwed on solidly to the body. See how they feel in your hand. Look at the thickness. Thin materials won't hold heat evenly. Thicker ones will be durable and withstand frequent washing. So, what are the basics? A good starter set should include three pans for making sauces and rice and an eight quart pasta or stock pot. Make sure to try the lids and see that they have a tight fit.

Then there are skillets, also known as frying pans or sauté pans. Again, get nonstick if you don't want to have a lot of stress. Methods for applying these coatings have improved over the years and are very affordable. Another advantage is that you can cut down the amount of fat you need to use. You'll need two sizes: an 8" skillet for things like eggs and single meals and a 12" for larger dishes like chicken, pork chops, chicken-fried steak.

What a crock! This is a slow cooker and can be very useful for one-dish meals. You can start cooking when you leave for work and your meal is ready when you get home.

A clay pot is a great investment. It's an ancient, easy and healthy way of cooking. I'll explain why later in this chapter.

Set of saucepans

Spaghetti or stock pot

Skillets

Crock Pot

Clay Pot

ESSENTIAL UTENSILS

Knives, pots and pans are fundamental items but there are other things you need to tool your kitchen, you can't live without.

- Mixing bowls, stainless steel or glass
- Measuring cup and spoons
- Garlic press
- Can opener
- Slotted spoon
- Spatula
- Whisk (that's not a card game)
- A baking sheet.
- Cutting boards; plastic ones are easier to clean and if wood splits, it can hold bacteria in the cracks. Get two boards, one for meat and one for vegetables.

As for appliances, a food processor does the most for the money but you can get away with a blender that has multiple functions. It does many of the same things that a food processor does, like chopping, liquefying, mixing and actually makes a better margarita. A steamer is another item you really need, especially for veggies. It leaves the flavors, color and texture intact and retains the most vitamins. Steamed food should never touch the water. The most practical and inexpensive kind is an expandable metal steamer. You may want to buy two.

ESSENTIAL UTENSILS GUIDE

 Blender

 Food Processor

 2 Plastic Cutting Boards

 4 Sided Hand Grater

 Potato Masher

 Utensil Set

 Measuring Spoons

 1 & 2 Cup Measuring Cups

 Steamer

 Casserole

 Can Opener

 Garlic Press

 Whisk

 Wooden Spoon

 Potato Peeler

 Mixing Bowls

 Colander

 Cookie Sheet

 Baking Pan

 Cork Screw

And the two most important kitchen utensils to help you cope in the kitchen!

 Bottle Opener

NO FEAR GROCERY SHOPPING

Okay. You've got the equipment you need to cook and some know-how, now you're ready to shop. Let's make it an adventure. I'm sure more than a few of you have gotten that dreaded call, "Can you pick up a few things for me on your way home?" You'd rather someone asked you to slay a dragon. You are about to embark on a trip to hostile territory…the supermarket. You enter without a map. Where are the breadcrumbs? They're not with the bread so where the heck are they? What about grated parmesan? Why isn't it the dairy section? It could be anywhere—so many aisles, so little time. Women can go right to any item like a guided missile. Invariably, you pick the wrong thing or are scolded for bringing home expensive things she didn't need.

All that's in the past. Face it—you're on your own. You have to shop. This is not the first time you've been shopping. You've had to buy staples like bread, coffee, eggs and beer. The difference between the sexes in the supermarket is strategy. Females have it; males don't. Women shop, they know what they need, they buy it. Men are impulse shoppers. They often ignore price. I'm here to save you from grocery shopping stress with some things I learned over the years I lived alone.

- Take it slow. Don't go in when you're rushed. Go to the same local store and get familiar with where things are. Supermarkets create floor plans like those theme parks that make you go through the gift shop to exit. Don't fall prey to that trick. Don't buy what they want you to buy, get what you need. Make a list. What a concept!
- If you can't find something, ask. Ask a woman. Some of them might be single!
- The latest innovation is the self-service check-out. It saves time but can be a

real pain since you have to scan each item yourself and do your own packing. If you have fruit or other things without a bar code it can get hairy. I'd rather have a person do that job who knows the price of avocados on sale that week, and I can't bag as fast as those packers do.

- Don't go during "rush hour" between 5:00 pm and 7:00 pm, when everybody is going home from work. Try to shop in the off hours. Most stores stay open at least until 11:00 pm. Shop late; it's much more civilized.
- My most important tip for the grocery store—don't go when you're hungry. The smell of baking bread is meant to whet your appetite. You'll go into the store for one or two staples and come out with a cart full of things you don't need. Take control of your supermarket experience and your wallet by shopping on a full stomach.
- I try to shop the outside aisles where they put the veggies, dairy and other "real food."

> **"The center of the supermarket is for boxed, frozen, processed, made-to-sit-on-your-shelf-for-months food. Ask yourself, 'If this food is designed to sit in a box for months, what is it doing inside my body?'"**
>
> —Morgan Spurlock, filmmaker and author, *Don't Eat This Book*

My goal is to show you how to cook for yourself with the added benefit of improving your eating habits. Choose foods that aren't heavily processed and packaged. Buy carrots with the tops on instead of the ones entombed in plastic and packed with preservatives to increase shelf life. The best tomatoes are grown in the summer and they have real taste, plus they're not waxed or sprayed or artificially made to look pretty. The term "food product" usually means that there is a small percentage of real food and the rest is filler. Whole foods are the best for you. Vegetables, fruits, nuts and grains have been found by the National Cancer Institute to play a major role in the prevention of cancer, heart disease and common digestive ailments.

I'm not going to tell you to stop eating meat but if you are what you eat, did you ever think that cows are also what they eat? Look for hormone-free beef and poultry. Don't be fooled by the term "free range" which conjures up images of happy grazing cows or chickens sitting on their nests in the open air. All it means is that the animals have access to the outside, but they can still be bio-engineered for fast growth. Buy organic products when you can. They have less pesticides and chemicals which could be the cause of some food allergies and may affect your overall health. The wisest choice in a meat purchase is definitely organic. You might spend more and eat less but that's not a bad thing since a major portion of artery-clogging fat comes from animal consumption. My absolute favorite place to purchase the highest quality organic meat online is Heritage Foods USA. Patrick Martins, the founder and former head of Slow Food USA founded Heritage in 2001 to encourage a market for high-quality, heritage breed meat products that are humanely raised by independent farmers. His dedication to this mission is unparalleled. You can order a wide variety of meats and even fish at www.heritagefoodsusa.com. It's amazing!

One thing you need to know about shopping is that there are alternatives to big supermarkets. I'm passionate about making righteous food choices. What the heck is that? It's a choice to buy food that does more than just satisfy your growling stomach. Supporting local growers is a giant step toward righteous food choice and you get a chance to know who's growing your food. If you buy from local producers you'll be always assured that food isn't transported and warehoused for days before you buy it. You can get tomatoes year round but how far did they travel and what preservatives were injected to get them from the grower to you? Produce from large supermarket chains can be trucked hundreds of miles before it hits your dinner plate. Shop at farmers' markets where you can find the freshest, widest selection of seasonal produce. Find one in your area from the Department of Agriculture at www.ams.usda.gov/farmersmarkets/index.htm.

If there is no farmers' market near you, there might be a community-supported agriculture group (CSA). This is similar to a food co-op where a local farmer grows food and delivers it to the member/shareholders. To find a CSA, log on to www.nal.usda.gov/afsic/csa/. Another alternative I have used is online produce companies. I like Seabreeze Organic Farm (www.stepheniefarm.com) but there are many more and surprisingly, the cost isn't much higher than regular organic grocery stores. One last thing, check out those "green supermarkets" and health food stores. Aside from your well-being, it's a great place to meet good, robust, nurturing babes. If you've never navigated the maze of the natural product aisles, ask one of these women for advice. You might improve both your eating habits and your love life. Later, when you're more expert, a man who has knowledge about food can also be a big turn-on for women.

THE WELL STOCKED PANTRY

You know how to navigate the store and maybe even get a date there. What's next is getting the basic items you need to start cooking and staples you want to have on hand. This avoids going grocery shopping every time you have to cook. You don't need to buy large quantities, especially with produce that's more perishable. Stay away from huge warehouse stores where you have to buy enough for an army battalion with each purchase. If you are price conscious, check out store brands and look on the shelf for pricing labels that will tell you the cost per unit for each item. You'll be surprised that some advertised "specials" are actually cheaper when the same items are purchased separately. It's okay to have a few convenience foods in the freezer for emergencies but if you have to buy them, go to a green market or look for the "health food" section in the supermarket. Natural food products have fewer chemicals and salt and more whole grains.

First, to start stocking your larder from scratch, let's look at seasonings, a major part of tasty cooking. There is more to life than salt, pepper and ketchup. Seasonings in the proper amount give ordinary dishes a flavor boost, turning them from bland to grand. Just so you know, a condiment is a sauce, an herb is a leaf and a spice comes from a bark, seed or flower.

I've divided the following lists into *must have* and *good to have*.

MUST HAVE CONDIMENTS	GOOD TO HAVE CONDIMENTS
Olive Oil	Chili sauce
Vegetable Oil	Honey mustard
Vinegar	Horseradish
Ketchup	Worcestershire Sauce
Mayonnaise or Vegenaise	Teriyaki sauce
Dijon Mustard	Chutney
Red Wine Vinegar	Sun Dried Tomatoes
Balsamic Vinegar	Capers
Vanilla	Poultry Seasoning
Honey	Salsa
Maple syrup	Hoisin Sauce
Cooking wine	Tabasco
Barbeque sauce	Spike
Soy sauce	Salad Dressing

MUST HAVE HERBS	GOOD TO HAVE HERBS
Basil	Tarragon
Dill	Mint
Oregano	Bay Leaf
Parsley flakes	Sage
Rosemary	Thyme
Cilantro	Chives

"Herbs and spices are the soul of your kitchen."

—Isabel Allende, Chilean writer, *Aphrodite: A Memoir of the Senses*

Herbs and spices work equally well in recipes whether fresh or dried, but fresh herbs should be added toward the end of the cooking time to preserve flavor. Whole spices and herbs, such as bay leaves or cloves, release flavor more slowly than ground. Grinding spices releases a more powerful essence. When doubling a recipe, only increase the amount of herbs and spices by one and a half.

MUST HAVE SPICES	GOOD TO HAVE SPICES
Salt*	Curry powder
Pepper	Crushed red pepper flakes
Sugar	Ginger
Cinnamon	Dried mustard
Garlic powder	Cloves (ground)
Onion flakes	Coriander seeds
Chili powder	Cumin
Nutmeg	Chinese five-spice powder
	Cajun spice
*Try to get Sea Salt	Paprika

GORDON SAYS: *Keep herbs and spices in a cool dark place. They usually are packaged in tins or plastic but glass is best to retain freshness. Most herbs are ground but I find that buying whole seeds and grinding them as needed packs more a powerful flavor punch.*

I'm not a fan of cans but here are some ones I usually have on hand. This may seem obvious, but don't buy canned goods that are dented because there is a possibility that they could be contaminated. Also, avoid any swollen tops which could be a sign of deadly botulism.

MUST HAVE CANNED GOODS	GOOD TO HAVE CANNED GOODS
Baked beans	Tomato paste
Tomatoes (whole/crushed)	Refried beans
Tomato sauce	Kernel corn
Tuna	Water chestnuts
Chicken broth	Artichoke hearts

MUST HAVE DRY GOODS	GOOD TO HAVE DRY GOODS
Beef bouillon cubes/ granules	Wild rice
Chicken bouillon cubes/ granules	Pancake mix
Flour	Raisins
Rice	Cooking spray
Pasta	Wondra©
Bread crumbs	Beans

GORDON'S TIP: *Get a set of wide-top canisters with tight lids for storing things like flour, coffee, rice, pasta and sugar. This will prevent pest invasion, especially in warm climates.*

You're probably wondering what the heck Wondra is. Most gravies and sauces call for flour in the form of a roux (butter-flour mixture) to thicken them, but if you don't know what you're doing, you'll get a lumpy mess. That's where Wondra comes in. It's flour that's finely ground so it dissolves quickly in water. A great shortcut.

STOCKING YOUR REFRIGERATOR

There is some comfort to opening the refrigerator and seeing more than old Chinese food cartons and beer, but actual food you can prepare or just eat when you're hungry. These are the basics which will feed you when all else fails:

- **Eggs**
- **Butter**
- **Milk**
- **Bread**
- **Bacon**
- **Deli Meats**
- **Sliced Cheese**
- **Lettuce**
- **Tomatoes**
- **Peanut Butter**
- **Jelly**

As I mentioned before, shop seasonally because food not only tastes better, it's less expensive. Keep some canned soups on hand and frozen items like chicken breasts which you can use in a variety of recipes. I really recommend fresh produce but frozen veggies are quick to use since they are usually trimmed, cut and pre-washed. It's okay to give yourself a break when you're in a time bind.

Another valuable item to stock is grated parmesan or Romano cheese. It adds flavor to many dishes, even non-Italian ones. Get it fresh-grated in the cheese section. Don't buy anything in a shaker that has heavy preservatives and no taste. Stay away from cheese you can pour. Cheddar can be used in a variety of entrees and is great for making burritos. Feta is a key ingredient in Greek salads and if you've never had goat cheese, you're in for a taste awakening. Remember that cheese is high in salt and fat so look for the "reduced-fat" kind if you're concerned about weight. Keep cheese refrigerated. You can use plastic wrap but wax paper is preferable for long term storage since cheese needs to breathe. Frozen cheese changes its texture but that won't be noticeable if you only use it for cooking. When a recipe calls for cheese, it's good to know which ones melt and I'm not talking about processed "cheese food" that never met a cow. You can use cheese to add richness to baked pasta, mashed potatoes, quiches, vegetable dishes and so much more. So here are some cheeses that melt in your mouth and in your recipe![1]

Melting		Non-Melting
Asiago	Gruyere	Fresh Mexican cheeses:
Bel Paese	Havarti	Queso Blanco, Queso Fresco
Brie	Jarlsberg	Ranchero, Cotija
Cheddar	Monterey Jack	Indian Paneer
Colby	Mozzarella	Cottage cheese
Edam	Muenster	Ricotta (except when baking it)
Fontina	Provolone	Goat cheese
Gouda	Swiss	Feta

"Cheese...milk's leap toward immortality."

—Clifton (Kip) Fadiman, American editor and writer

GORDON'S TIP: Parmesan and Pecorino cheeses are hard and should be finely grated before adding to any dish.

1. Finecooking.com - "How to Melt Cheese"

THE TRUTH ABOUT FRUITS AND VEGETABLES

If you want to know whether something is a fruit or a vegetable ask yourself this: Does it have seeds? If the answer is yes, it's a fruit, otherwise it's a veggie. The great tomato controversy has raged for years, but it is technically a fruit, as is a cucumber under this definition. These are botanically correct but we always find tomatoes in the vegetable section. Peas and beans are not vegetables but legumes because they grow in a pod! To confuse you, a legume can be a vegetable, but not all vegetables are legumes! Fruits and vegetables are seasonal. Today, you can get produce all year long but most of it is artificially ripened, colored and shipped from far-away places with preservatives to keep it looking fresh. To know what's in season in your area I recommend shopping at farmers' markets since you're sure to find the tastiest, best quality produce. Buying fruit in season is also less expensive. Here is a basic list to help you out.

	FRUITS	VEGGIES
Summer	berries, cherries, apricots, peaches, melons, plums, mangoes, grapes, tomatoes, eggplant	green beans, sweet corn, peppers, zucchini
Fall	apples, pumpkins, pears, persimmons	cauliflower, yams, broccoli, collards, Brussels sprouts
Winter	oranges, grapefruit, avocados	carrots, onions, acorn squash, turnips, cabbage, sweet potatoes
Spring	blackberries, strawberries, cucumbers	asparagus, lettuce, spinach, red radish, green onions, new potatoes

How can you tell if a fruit is ripe? You can use color, aroma, texture and even weight. Use your sense of smell for melons; they should have a full aroma. For pineapples, pull a green leaf from the center. If it pulls out easily, it's good to go. As fruits ripen, the substance that holds the cells together breaks down and becomes water-soluble which softens the flesh. Peaches, plums and nectarines don't have much flavor until they're ripe. Gently squeezing is a good test to see if they're soft. Eggplant should be firm to the touch. Avocado flesh will feel soft and the stems will pop off easily. Some fruits will ripen after they're picked, some won't. Here's a short list:

Berries, cherries, grapes, oranges, strawberries, grapefruit, watermelon, pineapple	Don't ripen after picking
Avocados	Ripen
Peaches, cantaloupe, honeydew, nectarines, apricots, blueberries, bananas	Ripen, Change color and texture
Apples, pears, papayas, mangoes, kiwi	Ripen and get sweeter

GORDON SAYS: *Fresh or organic tomatoes will keep at room temperature for about a week, but ones in the supermarket that have been refrigerated won't keep without cold.*

Another important part of stocking your refrigerator is to know how long fruits and vegetables will stay fresh. Freezing allows you to save seasonal produce for later use. Some may not be as good to eat when they're fresh but work well in recipes. When you freeze veggies, it's best to blanche first by immersing them in hot water and then plunging them into ice water. This preserves their crispness. In Chapter 2 we'll talk more about preparing food and meat storage, but here's a chart which will give you a good idea about the recommended storage times for fruits and vegetables.

VEGETABLE STORAGE	REFRIGERATOR	FREEZER (Blanched)
Artichokes	1 week	Not recommended
Asparagus	2-3 days	8-12 months
Beets, carrots	2 weeks	8-12 months
Beans, broccoli, peas	3-5 days	8-12 months
Cauliflower	1 week	8-12 months
Corn (husk on)	3-5 days	8-12 months
Green onions	3-5 days	Not recommended
Celery, cabbage, chilies, green beans	1 week	8-12 months
Green beans, tomatoes	1 week	8-12 months
Greens: collard, spinach, Swiss chard	3-5 days	8-12 months (blanched)
Lettuce and salad greens	1 week	Not recommended
Mushrooms	1-2 days	8-12 months (blanched)
Radishes	2 weeks	Not recommended
Small Summer squash	1-2 days	8-12 months
Large Winter squash (pumpkins)	Not recommended	Not recommended

FRESH FRUIT STORAGE	REFRIGERATOR	FREEZER
Apples	1 month	8-12 months
Apricots, grapes, nectarines	3-5 days	8-12 months
Avocados	3-5 days	8-12 months
Bananas, plantains	Not recommended	8-12 months
Berries, cherries	2-3 days	8-12 months
Grapefruit, lemons, limes, oranges	2 weeks	4-6 months
Guavas, papayas	1-2 days	8-12 months
Kiwis	3-5 days	4-6 months
Melons	1 week	8-12 months
Peaches, pears, plums	3-5 days	8-12 months
Pineapple	2-3 days	4-6 months

HOW TO READ A RECIPE

This first chapter would not be complete unless I taught you how to read a recipe. These are culinary roadmaps. I've made mine simple and geared them for novices. Preparation is straightforward with easy-to-follow directions. Remember, my goal is to teach you how cook for yourself, not make your head spin with a hundred recipes. There are lots of internet websites with all kinds of recipes available when you have the basics down. Here are my tips for what you need to know when you open any cookbook or recipe online.

- Read the recipe all the way through. Does it have very complicated instructions or ingredients you never heard of? Skip it. Keep it simple to start. Your cooking knowledge will broaden as you cook more. For now, stick to what you think you can handle. On Google, put "simple" or "easy" in the search and those recipes will come up!
- Check the serving size. Most recipes will feed four to six people. You can always increase it or cut it down. Make only what you need unless you're cooking ahead.
- Gather the ingredients. If you don't have every one, sometimes you can substitute, sometimes you can't. If you don't want to second guess, make a list of what's missing and buy it later or find another recipe.
- See what equipment you're going to need—pot, pan, skillet, baking dish, roasting pan, mixing bowls, measuring cups and spoons.
- Once you have the ingredients and tools, see how the food needs to be prepared—chopped, in chunks, diced, sliced, cut in strips, marinated—preparation can make or break a recipe.
- When you're ready to cook, follow the directions. Look at the order ingredients are added. Sometimes this will affect how things cook. See if the oven has to be pre-heated which takes between 10-15 minutes.

- The key to comedy and cooking is timing. If you're making a turkey dinner, don't cook the vegetables when you put the turkey in the oven. Consider how long things take to cook if you're making a whole dinner.

Here are a few other handy terms to know when you're reading a recipe:

- ✔ **Tbs or Tbsp** = Tablespoon
- ✔ **Tsp** = Teaspoon
- ✔ **Oz** = Ounce
- ✔ **C** = Cup
- ✔ **Season to taste** = You can add as much or as little as you want
- ✔ **Dash/Pinch** = Around 1/16th teaspoon
- ✔ **Mince** = Chop into tiny pieces
- ✔ **Beat** = Briskly stir with a spoon, fork or electric mixer
- ✔ **Grease** = Coat with a thin coat of oil, butter or cooking spray
- ✔ **Blend** = Mix together so you can't see the separate ingredients
- ✔ **Sear** = Cooking meat with high heat for a short time to seal in juices
- ✔ **Baste** = Spoon liquid over meat during cooking to avoid drying out

This next chart is one you'll find yourself consulting over and over again. I still do. I was cooking in a friend's kitchen and the recipe called for 1/3 cup of mayo but she only had measuring spoons. I checked the chart. The equivalent amount was 5 tablespoons plus 1 teaspoon. As many years as I've been cooking, even I didn't know that off the top of my head! See how much you know.

UNIT	DRY MEASURE	LIQUID MEASURE
1 teaspoon	1/3 tablespoon	1/6 fluid ounce
1 tablespoon	3 teaspoons	1/2 fluid ounce
2 tablespoons	1/8 cup (6 teaspoons)	1 fluid ounce
4 tablespoons	1/4 cup (12 teaspoons)	2 fluid ounces
1/8 cup	2 tablespoons	1 fluid ounce
1/4 cup	4 tablespoons	2 fluid ounces
1/3 cup	5 tablespoons + 1 teaspoon	2-2/3 fluid ounces
1/2 cup	8 tablespoons	4 fluid ounces
2/3 cup	10 tablespoons + 2 teaspoons	5-1/3 fluid ounces
3/4 cup	12 tablespoons	6 fluid ounces
7/8 cup	14 tablespoons	7 fluid ounces
1 cup	16 tablespoons	8 fluid ounces / 1/2 pint
2 cups	32 tablespoons	16 fluid ounces / 1 pint
4 cups	1 quart	32 fluid ounces
1 pint	32 tablespoons	16 fluid ounces / 1 pint
2 pints	1.0 quart	32 fluid ounces
8 pints	4 quarts	1 gallon / 128 fluid ounces

BASIC COOKING TECHNIQUES

Most men know how to turn on a stove. They can make breakfast and work a mean grill. That's a great start. I'm going to expand your kitchen knowledge by outlining some of the basic cooking techniques and how they work. Each method of cooking gives you a specific end result. Use this list as a guide and refer back to it when reading recipes.

Grilling/Broiling: Both use intense heat and are considered healthy cooking methods especially for meat because the fat drips out of the food. Grilling uses heat from below. Broiling uses heat from above. A barbeque is an outdoor grilling alternative to slaving over a hot stove.

Sautéing: (from the French word "jump") Cooking in an uncovered, flat-bottom pan using a small amount of fat over moderate to high heat. It's best to use oils that have a high smoke point like olive, vegetable or canola oils. Butter burns quickly. Items to be sautéed should be cut in uniform pieces to ensure they're all cooked evenly. Stir sparingly or shake the food with a back and forth motion to keep the food intact. Heat the pan before you add food. Dry off ingredients before you add them to this pan; this cuts down splatter when you're adding them or else keep Aloe Vera handy to soothe that certain oil burn.

You've seen those chefs on TV tossing their food from the frying pan into the air…that's called jumping. Guys, don't try this right out of the gate. It takes practice not to put the entire dish on the floor or cover yourself with food. If you want to look like Iron Chef, practice flipping with dried beans or rice. I've found mastering this really turns a woman on.

Deglazing: After you sauté and remove the food, there is residue left in the pan. To deglaze, add a small amount of room temperature liquid, like wine or stock. Scrap the bottom of the pan and cook on high heat to make a flavorful sauce.

Stir Frying: Chinese version of sautéing using sesame or peanut oil. It's best in a wok which has curved sides, but you can stir fry in any skillet.

Frying: Cooking in lots of hot fat, using heavy pans to distribute heat. Deep fried food is often covered in a batter and submerged in the fat. Pan fried food is half-submerged and usually has a flour or crumb coating. Coating food adds flavor and crispness. The exception is French fries which are cooked without a coating.

Roasting: Uses radiated heat in an oven. Cave men ate meat roasted over an open fire, i.e., hearth cooking. Today, we roast food in an open pan. Always pre-heat the oven before roasting. To see if the meat was done, my mother would poke it with a fork. If the end came out cold, it wasn't done. The best method is to use a meat thermometer to gauge the internal heat. After roasting, let the food sit for 5-10 minutes before slicing to allow it to stabilize.

Baking: Uses lower oven temperatures, even heat and is used for casseroles or food that is easily scorched, primarily those that contain flour.

Steaming: This is a gentle technique and healthiest because it keeps water soluble nutrients in the food. It also retains flavor since food is not immersed in water. Cutting food into small pieces will shorten the cooking time but you have to consider density. Carrots cook slower than mushrooms. Cover the pan tightly when steaming.

Blanching: Uses quick immersion in boiling water to pre-cook veggies. Remove from heat and plunge them in ice water to preserve crispness and color. If you want to intensify green color, put some salt in the water. If you want to intensify white, add lemon juice or vinegar. You can pre-cook veggies this way. When you get ready to serve them, submerge them in boiling water for a minute and they're ready to go.

Poaching: Different from blanching because food is cooked longer, temperature is lower and the liquid is well seasoned, like when you poach fish in wine.

Braising: A moist, low heat method in a covered container with liquid. Use for large, less tender cuts of meat such as pot roast. You can brown meat before braising to retain flavor. Slice across the grain, i.e., find the faint lines running through the meat and cut across the length of these lines, not in the same direction.

Stewing: Different from braising because food is cut into bite sized pieces and liquid completely covers it. Meat in stew is usually browned before the liquid is added.

Clay Pot: A slow cooking process, clay retains heat and it's porous so water is released during cooking. This creates natural juices which keep food moist. Clay also seals in the nutrients and seasonings for more flavor. Add vegetables to meat and you can make a whole meal. The water-soaked pot is placed in a cold oven at 425° for a few hours…the meat literally falls off the bone. I love it for tough beef cuts, ribs, chicken or pork.

Okay, you have your equipment, your groceries, your know-how and your nerve, so fire up your stove and let's start cooking!

"A kitchen condenses the universe."
—Betty Fussel, American author, *My Kitchen Wars*

NOTES:

CHAPTER 2

COOK FOR A DAY, EAT FOR A WEEK

et's face it. After a day battling bulls at the workplace, some days you're beat and just too damn tired to cook. The drive-through beckons. The temptation to bark your order into a speaker is overwhelming. Resist—there is another way. As a private chef, I worked for professional couples with children, busy executives and singles who didn't have time to make their own meals but wanted to eat well. I'm going to show you how to make good food in advance so you don't have to cook Monday through Friday. Cooking should be a stress reducer, not a chore. Before we get to the recipes, let's talk a little about how you keep and store food. Bird's Eye had the right idea when they made frozen convenience foods but had to add flavor-altering chemicals. You don't. Your dish can taste as good when you re-cook it as when you made it.

To freeze or not to freeze—that is the question. What foods should be frozen, how long will they last and how do you thaw them out? Food kept air-tight at Arctic cold temperatures can be stored for years. A mammoth frozen in Siberia was almost as fresh as the beef at your steak house kitchen when discovered. Jim Christie, a gold miner in the Yukon Territories, unearthed a 200,000-year-old bison but it was destroyed by oxygen and microbes before he could cook it. Your home freezer shelf life also relies mainly on how well you can keep air out. Remember that piece of meat you took out to cook that looked like elephant skin? It had freezer burn which comes from improper packaging. Here's what happens. When air gets inside the wrapping, water molecules escape and look for the coldest spot, usually the freezer wall. That part of the food then gets dehydrated which results in those grayish leathery spots on the surface. If there's not too much damage, you can cut away the burned sections before cooking. Even meats from the supermarket that are in plastic should be re-wrapped if not used in a few months. Wrap food in material designed for freezing. Freezer paper has a moisture-proof plastic coating inside. Regular plastic wrap and bags are usually too thin; buy the thicker ones marked for the freezer. Home freezers are not really meant for long-term storage. Food is properly frozen at a temperature range between -4 and +4 degrees Fahrenheit or -20 and -15 degrees Centigrade and can be monitored with a freezer thermometer available at most hardware stores.

Candidates for freezing are:
- leftovers that cannot be used immediately.
- seasonal fruits and vegetables.
- food you can prepare in quantity that still tastes good after a reasonable storage time.

Some foods shouldn't be frozen, like eggs in their shells, cheese, whipped or sour cream. Never put cans directly into the freezer.

How do you unfreeze food safely? Don't leave it on the counter because this slow method causes bacteria to grow on the first parts to thaw. If you have time, defrost food in the refrigerator. You can also use a microwave which usually has a chart listed for various food items by weight. Another method is to place food in a leak-proof plastic bag and immerse it in cold water. Be sure the bag is airtight and that you change the water every half hour since the frozen food makes it cold and prolongs the thaw. One of the most obscure but quickest ways to defrost is to place the unwrapped frozen food on an unheated heavy skillet. The metal will conduct room heat into the food. The heavier the pan, the more heat per minute it can conduct; flat foods, like steaks and chops, thaw fastest because they make direct contact. Don't defrost foods in a garage, basement, car, dishwasher, plastic garbage bag or outside in the sun. After thawing, refrigerate anything you won't use right away. On the following page is the recommended storage for refrigerator and freezer that gives you a run down of which common foods freeze well, which ones don't and how they can be frozen, stored and kept fresh.

THE STORAGE SAGA CONTINUES
FROM FRESH TO LEFTOVER

What about fresh food? Mother Nature didn't provide a mechanism to keep it that way for long. Believe it or not, fruits and veggies are alive. Keep bags open or punch holes in them—this lets food breathe. Mushrooms need to be in a paper bag; in plastic bags, you'll drown them in their own moisture. Never thought of yourself as a mass mushroom murderer have you? Don't store tomatoes, onions or garlic in the refrigerator but keep them in a cool, dry place. Don't put potatoes in the refrigerator because the cold causes starch to turn to sugar and that will darken them when cooked.

Are you confused by product dating? Here's the lowdown: "Sell by" is how long the store can put the product on display. "Best if used by" is how long the product will retain best flavor. "Use by" is the manufacturer's recommended date for peak quality. Looking back, I've used products after all these dates—I lived.

FOOD ITEM	REFRIGERATOR	FREEZER
Eggs		
Fresh, in shell	4 to 5 weeks	Don't Freeze
Raw yolks, whites	2 to 4 days	1 year
Hard Boiled	1 week	Not recommended
Deli Products		
Mayonnaise, (refrigerate after opening)	2 months	Don't freeze
Egg, chicken, tuna, ham, macaroni salads	3 to 5 days	Not recommended
Meat (Beef, Veal, Lamb, & Pork)		
Stew meats	1 to 2 days	3 to 4 months
Ground turkey, veal, pork, lamb	1 to 2 days	3 to 4 months
Steaks	3 to 5 days	6 to 12 months
Chops	3 to 5 days	4 to 6 months
Roasts	3 to 5 days	4 to 12 months
Bacon	7 days	1 month
Sausage, pork, beef, chicken or turkey	1 to 2 days	1 to 2 months
Smoked breakfast links, patties	7 days	1 to 2 months
Hot dogs, opened package	1 week	1 to 2 months
Hot dogs, unopened package	2 weeks	1 to 2 months
Lunch meats, opened package	3 to 5 days	1 to 2 months
Lunch meats, unopened package	2 weeks	1 to 2 months
Corned beef in pouch with pickling juices	5 to 7 days	Drained, 1 month
Ham, fully cooked, whole	7 days	1 to 2 months
Ham, fully cooked, half	3 to 5 days	1 to 2 months
Ham, fully cooked, slices	3 to 4 days	1 to 2 months

FOOD ITEM	REFRIGERATOR	FREEZER
Meat Leftovers		
Cooked meat & meat dishes	3 to 4 days	2 to 3 months
Gravy & meat broth	1 to 2 days	2 to 3 months
Cooked meat & meat dishes	3 to 4 days	2 to 3 months
Soups & Stews		
Vegetable or meat-added & mixtures	3 to 4 days	2 to 3 months
Fresh Poultry		
Chicken or turkey, whole	1 to 2 days	1 year
Chicken or turkey, parts	1 to 2 days	9 months
Giblets	1 to 2 days	3 to 4 months
Cooked Poultry, Leftover		
Fried chicken	3 to 4 days	4 months
Cooked poultry dishes	3 to 4 days	4 to 6 months
Pieces, plain	3 to 4 days	4 months
Pieces covered with broth, gravy	1 to 2 days	6 months
Chicken nuggets, patties	1 to 2 days	1 to 3 months
Fish & Shellfish		
Lean fish	1 to 2 days	6 months
Fatty fish	1 to 2 days	2 to 3 months
Cooked fish	3 to 4 days	4 to 6 months
Smoked fish	14 days	2 months
Fresh shrimp, scallops, crawfish, squid	1 to 2 days	3 to 6 months
Canned seafood, Pantry, 5 years	after opening 3 to 4 days	out of can 2 months

THE RICE RECIPE FOR SUCCESS

We'll start with rice which is a staple in the diet of one-half of the world's population. Rice cultivation dates back to China over 4,000 years ago. In early Chinese, the words for agriculture and rice were synonymous. The Greeks exported rice to Egypt in the 4th century. Early American colonists got rice by accident when a storm-damaged ship from Madagascar ended up in a Charleston, South Carolina harbor and a small gift of "golden seed rice" was given to a local planter. Rice was considered by many to be a symbol of fertility which is why people throw it at the bride and groom after a wedding. Rice is one of the easiest grains to digest so it's a good choice if you have a food allergy. It's also a source of protein which your body needs.

Rice is rice, right? Wrong. There are different types of rice. You may have eaten rice that's too wet, too dry or too lumpy. Have no fear—you can make great rice the very first time. First, let's look at the different varieties.

Brown Rice: All rice has an inedible husk. When that husk is removed but left in its natural state, the result is brown (unpolished) rice.

White Rice: It's refined by having the bran and germ removed then polished to a smooth sheen.

Long Grain Rice: It's exactly that—rice with thin, pointed grains.

Basmati Rice: A long grain variety with a superior flavor.

Jasmine Rice: It's long grain, a little sticky and used in Asian cooking; also called "Fragrant Rice."

Risotto, Arborio: Shorter, plumper grains. This takes more attention while cooking but the end result is worth it.

Short Grain Rice: It's stickier and the kind used in sushi.

Rice You Cook In A Minute: It's partially cooked after milling and only needs to absorb water. It's the white bread of the rice world; the flavor is dull and flat. Some labels say "vitamin enriched." I wouldn't drop my One-A-Day for it.

Wild Rice: It's not even rice. It's the seed of a grass grown in the swamps of North America. Sounds gross but tastes great. It has a subtle nutty flavor and takes longer to cook, about 50 minutes. The seeds burst and split slightly.

GORDON'S TIP: *Store uncooked rice in an airtight container in a cool dry place and it will keep at least a year.*

I like to use the more flavorful long grain white rice like Basmati or Jasmine which makes a fluffy, drier dish. Most people cook rice in a saucepan but you can also make it in a frying pan. The key is to have a very tight lid.

BASIC RICE FORMULA:

1 part rice to 2 parts liquid.

1 cup of rice is 3 average servings

"I like rice. Rice is great if you're hungry and want 2,000 of something."

—Mich Ehrenborg, French author (1783)

GORDON SAYS: *For more flavorful rice, use chicken stock. You can make your own and freeze it in an ice cube tray to use later. You can also buy liquid stock or granulated bouillon.*

NICE AND EASY RICE

Bring 2 cups of chicken stock and 1 cup rice to a boil.

(You can put in a tablespoon of butter for flavor.)

Stir, cover and cook for 15 minutes on a low flame.

Remove from heat. Water will be absorbed.

Fluff with a fork and serve.

BASIC RICE PILAF

INGREDIENTS:

3 tablespoons butter

1 cup Basmati or white rice

2 cups chicken stock (or vegetable stock)

1 small red bell pepper (chopped)

1 small onion (chopped)

1 clove garlic (chopped)

1/2 teaspoon salt

1/4 teaspoon pepper

Serves 4

DIRECTIONS:

1. Melt butter. Sauté onions & peppers over medium heat until soft.

3. Add rice and garlic. Stir until rice is coated and turns light brown.

4. Add stock, cover and bring to a boil.

5. Turn heat to low flame or low setting.

6. Simmer for about 20 minutes or until the liquid is absorbed.

GORDON'S WARNING: *Don't keep stirring rice during cooking. This breaks down the grain and you'll get a starchy sticky mess. Don't lift the cover! It stops the cooking process.*

Cooked rice will keep for one week if it's covered and refrigerated. It can also be frozen alone or in other foods for several months in freezer containers. One cup of cooked white basmati rice has only 103 calories and does not have any cholesterol, sodium or fat (unless you add it). There is no gluten which makes it great for those who can't eat wheat. The reason that rice gets hard in the refrigerator is because the starch reverts to its insoluble state but you can use it again in soups, stir fry, a quick casserole, or my favorite, fried rice. You can freeze plain rice in bags but it needs a liquid to reconstitute. Here are a few ways you can reheat cooked rice:

Oven: Mix rice with melted butter to moisten. Cover with foil. Heat at 250° until hot.

Stovetop: Add 2 tablespoons of water to each cup of cooked rice. Cook over very low flame. Stir occasionally until heated.

Microwave: Add 2 tablespoons of water to each cup of cooked rice. Cover with plastic wrap or a wet paper towel. Cook 1-2 minutes depending on microwave strength, until heated.

Steamer: Place rice in steamer in a saucepan with water to reach the steamer. Cover, boil water and steam about 3 minutes or until heated through.

> ## "The most remarkable thing about my mother is that for thirty years she served the family nothing but leftovers. The original meal has never been found."
> —Calvin Trillin, Humorist, food writer, *The Tummy Trilogy*

Most likely Calvin's mother made some of those dishes with cooked rice since it has so many variations. It may even be better as an ingredient in a leftover entrée than a side dish. This next recipe is great for using leftover chicken!

LEFTOVER CHICKEN & RICE

INGREDIENTS:

1 cup leftover rice (any kind)

2 tablespoons butter or 2 frozen chicken stock cubes

1 cup leftover chicken*

*Substitute chicken with leftover beef, pork, shrimp, veggies

Serves 4

DIRECTIONS:

1. Sauté 1 cup of leftover chicken in 2 tablespoons of butter until heated. For lower calories, use 2 frozen stock cubes or 2 tablespoons chicken stock.
2. Put rice in a saucepan with 2 tablespoons of water.
3. Cover rice and heat on low until heated.
4. To serve, toss chicken and rice together or place chicken on top of a bed of rice on each plate.

How many times have you been stuck with leftover white rice from a Chinese restaurant? Here's how to make homemade fried rice for a side dish or a whole meal. Restaurant leftovers are great because they use sticky rice, but any rice can work in this recipe.

FRIED RICE – TWICE AS NICE

INGREDIENTS:

1 cup leftover rice (any kind)

2 tablespoons vegetable oil

1/2 cup leftover chicken*, chopped

2 tablespoons soy sauce**

1 egg, beaten

1 medium scallion***, chopped

*Substitute leftover beef, pork, shrimp, veggies
**Use reduced sodium soy sauce
***Substitute onions for scallions.

Serves 2

DIRECTIONS:

1. Place 1 tablespoon oil in a fry pan. Add the egg and scramble until cooked. Remove egg & set aside.
2. Add more oil and cook scallions over high heat for one minute.
3. Add the chicken, rice and soy sauce. Stir over high heat for 2 minutes or until heated through.
4. Add egg and mix thoroughly.

SIMPLE SPANISH RICE

INGREDIENTS:

2 tablespoons, olive or vegetable oil

1/2 green pepper, diced

1 medium onion, chopped

2 garlic gloves, minced

1 teaspoon salt

Pepper to taste

1 cup leftover rice

1½ cups leftover ground beef or ground turkey *

1 small can of tomato sauce

*Can also use leftover hamburgers or meatloaf

Serves 4

DIRECTIONS:

1. Heat oil in a frying pan for a minute.
2. Add onion, garlic, salt and pepper. Cook until soft.
3. Add ground meat * and tomato sauce. Heat through.
4. Add rice. Heat several more minutes until hot.

If you don't have any leftover ground meat follow the instructions below.

Heat oil in a fry pan. Add 1/2 lb ground meat and break up with a fork while cooking until it's crumbled and well done. Salt & pepper to taste.

Drain fat from pan & set aside. Add cooked meat to softened pepper, onion and garlic.

"Life is a combination of magic and pasta."

—Frederico Fellini, Italian film director

PASTA

Pasta is versatile, easy to cook and has tons of variations. It's gotten a bad rap in this "no-carb" crazy world but the fact is, a whole cup of cooked pasta only has 170 calories, has little saturated fat or sugar and is high in selenium, iron and thiamin. Over 80% of the calories in pasta come from complex carbohydrates the body needs; the rest are protein. A cup of cooked pasta has more protein than a cooked egg. The rich sauces are what can add weight, not to mention the amount of garlic bread consumed.

Pasta wasn't brought to Italy from China by Marco Polo as the story goes. It dates back to the Etruscans in 400 B.C. but the first documented recipe came from a cookbook written in 1,000 A.D. by a Sicilian Chef, Martino Corna: *The Art of Cooking Vermicelli And Macaroni*. The first historical references to production of dried pasta were in Palermo. The upper classes didn't eat pasta until the fork was popularized. The two tine version was used for holding meat down. Some believe the King of Naples' chamberlain came up with the four tine modern version. The first pasta factory in the U.S. opened in Brooklyn in 1848. What's the proper etiquette for eating pasta? Many people use a spoon to twirl their spaghetti but that's not the custom in Italy where a reasonable amount is wound on the fork held against the plate. Never slurp the strands up to your mouth. Italians say that the character of a man can be determined by the way he eats spaghetti.

The key ingredient of pasta is wheat. Look for 100% semolina or Durham wheat because it will retain shape and firmness best during cooking. Noodles are pasta products made with egg solids which give them that yellow color. Why are there so many shapes? Isn't pasta all the same? Nope. The shapes determine how sauce will stick to the pasta. Some are best with thin sauces; other shapes have ridges which will catch chunkier sauces. The following chart gives you an idea of what shape goes best with what type of sauce.

SPAGHETTI: Long, thin and round, this is the most well known pasta shape. It's ideal with any type of sauce. Not good for pasta salads. Spaghettini and capellini (angel hair) are thinner varieties of spaghetti. Use a more liquid sauce that distributes evenly. Thick or cream sauces, like Alfredo, will make it gum up.

Spaghetti

PENNE: A smooth tubular pasta that works well with red, white and cream based sauces.

Penne

PENNE RIGATI: Same shape but with ridges. Use heavier sauces, like meat, tomato or vegetable.

Rigatone

ZITI: This is a type of smooth penne with squared off ends.

RIGATONI: This is a medium tube-shaped pasta with ridges. It works well with sauces that cling to the grooves: meat, tomato, pesto. Good for baked dishes.

Farfalle

FARFALLE: This bow-tie shaped pasta actually means "butterfly." It's best with chunky sauces and great for pasta salads or vegetable sauces.

Fusilli

FUSILLI: Spiral shaped pasta, once handmade by twisting it around a knitting needle. Heavy sauce and chunky sauces cling to the spirals.

CONCHIGLIE: Shells, available in various sizes. The largest can be stuffed. This is great for chunky sauces which adhere well to the shape.

Conchiglie

ELBOWS: This macaroni is good for any type of sauce. Use for pasta salad, soup, baked dishes, macaroni and cheese.

Elbows

FETTUCINE: Long, flat ribbon which works well with heavy sauces.

LINGUINE: A 1/3 thinner version of the flat ribbon. Works better with a more liquid sauce, like clam sauce. Cut in pieces and add to soups.

Fettucini

"Everything you see, I owe to spaghetti."

—Sophia Loren, Italian actress

Now I'll give you some of my personal tips for cooking perfect pasta.

WATER: Pasta needs lots of water—about 4 quarts for every pound. Why? Pasta releases a starchy substance. If you don't have enough water to dilute it, the water will thicken and the pasta won't cook evenly. It will also be gooey and have a starchy taste.

COOK: Always bring the water to a rolling boil, then add the pasta. Return the water to a rolling boil and keep it there. Never simmer cooking pasta. You need that high heat to prevent the pasta from sticking together. Don't cover the pot or it will boil over. Don't add oil to the water unless you're cooking large pasta, like lasagna.

SALT: Salt the water before you put in the pasta. Use a few tablespoons. This won't make the water boil faster but does add flavor. If you have a health problem, you can leave the salt out.

STIR: Use a wooden spoon to keep the pasta moving so that it cooks evenly and doesn't stick together.

TIME: Packages have cooking times; I don't rely on them. If you want to use the package time, add 2 minutes since they begin timing after the water restarts boiling. Fresh pasta takes much less time to cook. Don't mix different types of pastas in one pot since they will have different cooking times.

TEST: The best way to tell if pasta is done is to test it. Timing begins after the water restarts to boil. Depending on the shape, cooking can be from 3-13 minutes. Take out a piece of pasta, bite it. Pasta should be tender and firm or 'al dente' (to the tooth). Look at the center. If there is some white left, cook just a minute more. Don't forget, pasta is still cooking when it's out of the pot so don't overcook it.

DRAIN: Pour the pasta into a colander in the sink. Watch that hot water splash! Pick up the colander to drain the excess water. You can keep some of that water if you need to thin out your sauce. Immediately toss pasta with sauce so that it doesn't become one big lump. DO NOT rinse unless you are making pasta to save for later or if you are making a pasta salad. DO RINSE lasagna noodles or you won't be able to separate them

GORDON'S WARNING: *If you're using cooked pasta in a baked dish, drain when you see that white line. It must be firm because it will cook in the oven.*

COOKING PASTA TO SAVE: Pasta will keep in the refrigerator in a plastic bag for 3-4 days. After you drain it, rinse with cold water to stop it from cooking. Drain again. Let it cool. Toss with a few teaspoons of oil. Store in air-tight plastic bags.

REHEATING PASTA: Boil water. Drop in the pasta for a few minutes, then drain. Put sauce on immediately. To microwave, add more sauce if it's too dry, cover with plastic wrap leaving one corner open. Cook on "high" for one to three minutes depending on the amount of pasta you have.

HOW MUCH TO SERVE: The rule of thumb is 4 ounces per person if it's a main dish. One cup of dried pasta is about 2 ½ cups cooked elbow macaroni, shells, rotini, cavatelli, wheels, penne, or ziti. Four ounces of uncooked or a 1-inch diameter bunch of dry pasta will equal 2 cups cooked spaghetti, angel hair, vermicelli or linguine.

PASTA SAUCES TO SERVE AND SAVE

These are some sauces which can be made ahead and saved in the refrigerator or frozen. I'll start with a basic, meatless tomato sauce. Marinara got its name from the sailors who brought tomatoes to Italy. This basic sauce can be varied by adding meat, vegetables or fish. It's great for dishes that need to be baked like chicken parmigiana or baked ziti. I use fresh tomatoes when they are in season. Marinara sauce will keep for about a week in a covered container or frozen for 6 months.

BASIC MARINARA SAUCE

INGREDIENTS:

28 oz can whole tomatoes (Italian plum are best) OR

2 lbs fresh tomatoes, peeled, seeded and chopped

6 oz can tomato paste

1/4 cup olive oil

3 medium garlic cloves chopped

2 teaspoons parsley flakes

1/2 cup fresh basil chopped (remove stems) OR 2 tablespoons dried basil

1 teaspoon salt

1/4 teaspoon black pepper

Serves 4

DIRECTIONS:

1. Chop tomatoes in a blender.
2. Heat the oil. Place the garlic in a skillet. Cook on low heat for 1-2 minutes.
3. Add tomato paste and 1 paste can full of water.
4. Add the chopped tomatoes, basil, parsley, salt, pepper.
5. Simmer (medium heat) for 20 minutes. Add water if it's too thick.
6. Toss with 1 lb of pasta & serve.

MARINARA SAUCE VARIATIONS

- Remove meat from 4 sweet Italian sausages. In a skillet, brown meat in 1/4 cup red wine or in 2 tablespoons of olive oil, crumbling with a fork while cooking. Drain off the fat and add to the marinara sauce.
- Add raw, deveined shrimp, fresh lobster or drained canned tuna to the sauce. Cook for 10 minutes more.
- Add cooked vegetables and simmer 5 more minutes.

If you are using fresh tomatoes in sauce, here's how you peel and seed them.

HOW TO PEEL & SEED TOMATOES

1. Bring a saucepan 3/4 filled with water to a rolling boil.
2. Make five 1/4" light slits in the tomato skins.
3. Plunge the tomatoes into the boiling water for 1 minute.
4. Remove the tomatoes and peel when cool.
5. Cut the tomatoes in half.
6. Gently squeeze each half so the seeds drip out.

GORDON SAYS: *How you prepare tomatoes is up to you. If you like a chunkier sauce, chop by hand or use blender on "chop." If you like a smooth sauce, blend on "high" or on the "puree" setting. You can also add 1/4 cup of red wine to the sauce when cooking for a hearty, robust flavor.*

This next recipe comes from Reparata's personal kitchen. She learned it at her mother's knee growing up in Brooklyn, New York. Rep is famous for her meatballs and this recipe uses that seasoning as a basis for an authentic, delicious Italian meat sauce or gravy as it's called in her home town. You'll have to wait for the next book to get her legendary meatball recipe!

REPARATA'S "BROOKLYN" MEAT SAUCE

INGREDIENTS:

MEAT

1 pound ground beef (not too lean)

3 cloves copped garlic

1 egg, beaten

1/4 cup, fresh grated Pecorino Romano or Parmesan cheese

2 tablespoons dried parsley flakes

1 teaspoon salt

1/4 teaspoon pepper

3 tablespoons olive oil

SAUCE

28 oz can Italian plum tomatoes

6 oz can tomato paste

3 medium garlic cloves, chopped

2 teaspoons parsley flakes

1/2 teaspoon oregano

1/2 cup fresh basil chopped (remove stems) OR 2 tablespoons dried basil

1 teaspoon salt

1/4 teaspoon black pepper

1 cup water*

*You can use 1/2 cup water and 1/2 cup dry red wine

Serves 4

DIRECTIONS:

MEAT

1. Mix all the ingredients together by hand or with a food processor with a plastic blade until well blended.

2. Heat the oil in a skillet on medium. Add the meat and crumble with a fork until browned.

3. Drain off the fat and set aside.

SAUCE

1. Puree tomatoes in a blender or food processor.

2. Pour the pureed tomatoes into a large saucepan. Add tomato paste and 1 cup of water.

3. Add the garlic, parsley flakes, basil, oregano, salt, pepper and wine.

4. Add the crumbled, cooked ground beef.

5. Simmer on low heat for 1½ hours. Stir occasionally.

6. Toss with 1 lb of cooked pasta & serve.

These next recipes are simple sauces which have short prep time. You can use this next one on almost any shaped pasta in the chart except thin spaghetti or capellini. Pesto can give your pasta a gourmet feel. The basic ingredient is fresh basil. Most supermarkets now carry fresh herbs. If you live in a temperate climate you can grow them in your garden or in pots. The best thing is that this sauce will keep in the refrigerator and you can freeze it.

BASIC PESTO SAUCE

INGREDIENTS:

1 cup packed basil (stems removed)

1/4 cup pine nuts or walnuts

3 garlic cloves, chopped

1/2 cup Pecorino Romano or parmesan cheese

1/2 cup olive oil

Serves 4

DIRECTIONS:

1. Place all the ingredients and 1 tablespoon of oil into a blender or food processor.
2. Blend 5 seconds.
3. With the machine running, slowly drizzle in the remaining oil.
4. Blend until the mixture has the consistency of thick cream.
5. Toss with 1 lb of cooked pasta & serve.

GORDON'S TIP: *Refrigerate pesto in a jar or container. Cover the surface with a thin film of olive oil on top to stop it from turning dark green. Freeze in a container. For single portions, freeze in an ice cube tray then transfer the cubes to a plastic freezer bag. Thaw in the refrigerator or defrost in a microwave on low. Don't overheat.*

"Fettuccini Alfredo is macaroni and cheese for adults."

—Mitch Hedberg, American comedian

QUICK CLASSIC ALFREDO SAUCE

INGREDIENTS:

1/4 stick or 8 tablespoons butter

1 cup heavy cream

1/2 cup grated parmesan cheese, room temperature

1/4 teaspoon salt

Pepper to taste

Pinch of nutmeg

Serves 4

DIRECTIONS:

1. Melt butter in a fry pan over low heat.
2. Add cream slowly and stir until heated through and starts to thicken.
3. Gradually add parmesan, salt, pepper & nutmeg.
4. Continue stirring until blended and hot.
5. Toss with 1 lb of cooked pasta & serve

Low-cal Substitution: Use only 2 tablespoons of butter. Replace creams with reduced fat milk. Add 2 tablespoons of Wondra® flour to thicken the sauce.

When you walk through the door and you're really hungry, here's a simple quick Italian classic for garlic lovers, *Pasta Al Olio*.

GARLIC & OIL SAUCE

INGREDIENTS:

1/3 cup olive oil

3 large garlic cloves, minced

1 tablespoon chopped parsley

2 tablespoons white wine*

Salt & pepper to taste.

*You can use stock

Serves 4

DIRECTIONS:

1. Heat oil in a saucepan or small skillet.
2. Add garlic and cook until browned.
3. Add white wine and parsley.
4. Simmer on low heat for 10 minutes.
5. Toss with 1 lb of cooked pasta & serve.

Variations:

Add 2 tablespoons of capers with the parsley.

Add 5 chopped anchovy fillets with the parsley.

Replace garlic with one medium onion, sliced very thin.

SWEET PEPPER SAUCE

INGREDIENTS:

3 peppers green, yellow, red or a combination, seeded and cut into thin strips.

3 garlic cloves, minced

2 tomatoes, diced*

1/4 cup olive oil

1 cup chicken or vegetable stock

1/2 teaspoon salt

1/4 teaspoon black pepper

1/4 teaspoon salt

You can use peeled & seeded tomatoes. See earlier instructions.

Serves 4

DIRECTIONS:

1. Remove tops of peppers and the seeds. Cut into strips.
2. Heat oil in a fry pan. Add garlic and lightly brown. Do not burn.
3. Add tomatoes onions, salt & pepper. Simmer for 5 minutes.
4. Add peppers. Cover and cook until vegetables are soft, about 10 more minutes.
5. Add water, stock or white wine if sauce is too thick.
6. Toss with 1 lb of cooked pasta & serve

For a smoother sauce, place the sauce in a blender and puree. Return to pan and gently re-heat for 5 more minutes.

For added flavor, remove meat from 3 sweet Italian sausages and fry with peppers. Crumble meat with a fork as it cooks until browned.

Roasted peppers are great in this dish or on sandwiches. Here's how to make them.

ROASTED PEPPERS

- Cut peppers in half. Remove seeds.
- Place peppers on a baking sheet, skin side up, in a 400° oven for 30-45 minutes or until the skins blister and blacken. You can also broil them for 10-20 minutes.
- Remove and place peppers in a covered bowl or Ziploc. Let stand 10 minutes for steam to loosen the skin. When cool, peel off the blackened skins.
- To use later, put them in a jar with olive oil and a few cut up garlic cloves.

For vegetarians, or just for weight control, you can make sauces with a variety of vegetables like broccoli, peas, cauliflower, zucchini or rapini. Here is a simple recipe from Reparata's kitchen that is great served with spaghetti or farfalle hot, as a main course, or cold as a pasta salad.

PASTA WITH BROCCOLI

INGREDIENTS:

1 head fresh broccoli (or 1 bag frozen)

1/3 cup olive oil

1/3 cup water

5 garlic cloves, chopped

1/2 teaspoon salt

1/4 teaspoon black pepper

2 tablespoons white wine, optional

1 lb cooked pasta

Serves 4

DIRECTIONS:

1. Break broccoli flowers from the stem.*

2. In a large saucepan, place the broccoli, olive oil, water, garlic, salt and pepper.

3. Simmer on medium heat for 30 minutes, stirring occasionally until broccoli turns light green and has the consistency of a thick sauce.

4. Turn into a bowl and toss with the pasta.

*Frozen broccoli florets can work in a pinch.

"If your mother cooks Italian food, why should you go to a restaurant?"

—Martin Scorsese, American film director

THE INCREDIBLE EDIBLE POTATO

What do you really know about potatoes? There's a popular myth that the carbohydrates will make you fat. In Chapter 4, the no-carb myth is debunked and you'll see that gaining weight is a combination of factors. Potatoes are not high in calories; it's what you put on them. Smear a potato with sour cream, butter, top with bacon and you'll find the pounds creeping up. Another misconception is that potatoes have no nutritional value. The fact is this vegetable contains many essential nutrients needed for a healthy diet.

Also in Chapter 4, I'll go into detail about how to decipher a food label. Here's one you might find on a potato. There is no fat, cholesterol or sodium in a potato. Fiber promotes digestion and may help decrease the risk of colon cancer and heart disease. Vitamin C is a powerful antioxidant that protects your body's cells, boosts the immune system to help prevent infection and even keeps gums healthy. Food that's high in potassium and low in sodium may also reduce your risk of high blood pressure and stroke. A potato has four grams of protein which helps muscle strength. It has complex carbohydrates to provide energy for the body.

Nutrition Facts

Serving Size 1 potato (148g)

Amount Per Serving

Calories 100

	% Daily Values*
Total Fat 0g	0%
Saturated Fat 0g	0%
Trans Fat 0g	
Cholesterol 0mg	0%
Sodium 0mg	0%
Total Carbohydrate 26g	9%
Dietary Fiber 3g	12%
Sugars 3g	
Protein 4g	8%

Vitamin C 45%	•	Calcium 2%
Iron 6%	•	Thiamin 8%
Riboflavin 2%	•	Niacin 8%
Vitamin B6 10%	•	Folate 6%
Phosphorus 6%	•	Magnesium 6%
Zinc 2%		

*Percent Daily Values are based on a 2,000 calorie diet. Your Daily Values may be higher or lower depending on your calorie needs.

		Calories	2,000	2,500
Total Fat		Less than	65g	80g
Sat Fat		Less than	20g	25g
Cholesterol		Less than	300mg	300mg
Sodium		Less than	2400mg	2400mg
Total Carbohydrate			300g	375g
Dietary Fiber			25g	30g

SO MANY POTATOES, SO LITTLE TIME

Before we look at the potato varieties, do you know why they're also called "spuds?" The theory I like best is that it comes from the spudder tool used to dig them up. Potatoes are tubers (roots) and there are hundreds of varieties harvested all over the world. Colors can be dirt brown, red, yellow, gold, purple and white with thick or thin skins. In the U.S., the russet is the most common; it's brown and comes in small, medium or large. My personal preferences are Yukon Gold and Fingerling. They have a natural buttery flavor which is good if you're concerned about weight. The skin on these is smooth so you can mash them without peeling. That's important because many of the nutrients are in the skin or just under it; when you peel the potato or boil it you lose some of that nutrition. A potato has eyes which are actually where they would sprout if they continued to grow. It's best to remove the eyes especially if they have any green parts that contain bitter tasting, toxic solanine. Gouging them out with a small paring knife will take care of it. Let's look at a few of the varieties which are most commonly found in the produce section.

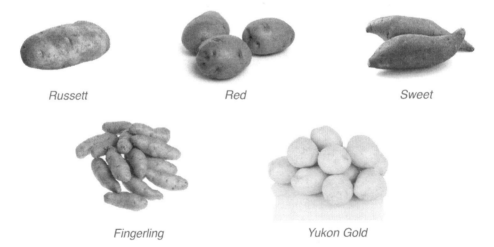

Russett *Red* *Sweet*

Fingerling *Yukon Gold*

Are a yam and a sweet potato the same thing? They're not. A true yam is a Dioscorea root and not grown as a food product in the U.S. In the early 1900's, sweet-potato promoters used the word "yam" to identify the deeper orange, moist-fleshed varieties. The potato was first cultivated by the Incas in Peru around 200 B.C. The Spanish brought it to Europe in the 16th century. Spuds arrived in Jamestown Virginia in 1621. It was Thomas Jefferson who brought French fries from Paris to the White House. Cornelius Vanderbilt complained that his potatoes were cut too thick. His offended chef sliced them paper-thin, fried them and the potato chip was born.

What should you look for when buying potatoes? They should be firm without cuts, cracks or discoloration and have a fairly regular shape for easy peeling. Avoid ones that are sprouted, shriveled or have green on the skin; that toxic solanin could have penetrated the flesh. Most store bought potatoes go through a wash process but I'd rinse them again before cooking.

GORDON SAYS: *Don't refrigerate potatoes. They develop sugar which darkens them. Too much light turns them green.*

BASIC COOKING METHODS

The most popular way to serve potatoes is baked; mashing baked potatoes gives them a subtle roasted flavor. You can use leftovers for a variety of other dishes. Don't boil large potatoes whole because it takes longer to cook and more nutrients will be lost. Cut up large potatoes if you steam or boil them.

BOILING POTATOES

Use this method for mashing or making salads

1. Wash potatoes under cold running water. Use a soft brush if you have one.
2. Cut 5-7 large potatoes into chunks. Leave smaller potatoes whole. You can leave the skin on.
3. Place potatoes in a saucepan with a tight-fitting lid in about 2" of water.
4. Bring water to a boil.
5. Simmer 30-40 minutes or until soft when pierced with a fork.
6. Drain and let cool before removing skins, if left on. Small potatoes do not need peeling for further preparation.

For more flavor, boil in stock or add garlic to the water.
For a sweeter flavor, add milk to the water.

GORDON'S TIP: *Put a quarter of a lemon in the cooking water to keep the potatoes from breaking up...advice directly from the Idaho Potato Commission!*

STEAMING POTATOES*

Place cut potatoes, peeled or with skins on, in a steamer in a saucepan with water just below the basket.

Add salt to the water to enhance the flavor.

Cover and steam 40 minutes or until tender. Drain and let cool.

Steaming retains more nutrients. Use for mashing or making potato salad.

BAKING POTATOES*

Pre-heat oven to 400°.

Wash the potatoes. Pierce the skin of each one in 8-10 places with a fork. This allows team to escape during cooking and keeps the potato from bursting.

Place them on the oven rack to distribute heat evenly.

Bake 40-55 minutes or until tender when pierced with a fork.

Remove and serve. To open, make a dotted line lengthwise with a fork.

Press potato at both ends gently to fluff. Watch out for the steam!

For crispier skin, rub with a light coat of vegetable or olive oil or butter. Don't wrap potatoes in foil; it holds moisture.

GORDON'S WARNING: *Don't use a knife to open a baked potato, it flattens the surface. Don't leave leftover baked potatoes out overnight and think you can eat them the next day. Baked potatoes must be refrigerated since they are quick to grow micro-organisms.*

QUICK BAKED*

1. Wash potatoes. Cut in half length-wise. Brush cut side lightly with oil.
2. Grease a baking sheet. Place potatoes, face down.
3. Bake at 350° for 25 minutes or until tender when pierced with a fork.

*For 1-2 servings, you can use a toaster oven. Be sure it has an oven insert.

MICROWAVE BAKED*

1. Spread paper towels on the microwave bottom.
2. Place potatoes 1" apart. Pierce skin in 8-10 places.
3. Microwave on HIGH for 8 minutes.
4. Test for doneness with a fork. If soft, remove and wrap in foil.**
5. Let stand for 5 minutes before serving. Remove wrap and serve.

*Not recommended for mashing.
**Never put any foil-wrapped object in a microwave.

How do you make mashed potatoes so they're not lumpy, gummy, watery, pasty and heavy but smooth, creamy, flavorful, fluffy and light? There is a way and there is science behind it which we'll talk about in a minute. First, let's look at some of the tools you can buy to mash potatoes.

I use the one on the right. It's inexpensive and the handle has a good feel. One thing you must know when mashing a potato. You have to mash up and down. Why? Potatoes cells have gelatinous starch granules. If you mash sideways or stir, you're going to release those babies into the mixture and get glue. Square holes are best because the potato flesh is extruded through and doesn't crush the cell walls. Never put potatoes in the food processor thinking that will make them smooth and creamy. The blades cut through the cells and you're guaranteed to have a gummy mess. Mashing is good for you. You can take out the day's frustrations on the potatoes and reduce your stress. One pound, which is about 3 medium-sized potatoes, will make 2 cups of cooked mashed potatoes. Everyone has a favorite way to make mashed potatoes—here's mine. I prefer Yukon Gold or Fingerling in this recipe but you can use Russet or any other kind of potato.

MANLY MASHED POTATOES

INGREDIENTS:

2 lbs boiled Yukon Gold or Fingerling or 4 large Russet potatoes

2 teaspoons salt or to taste

6 tablespoons soft butter in pieces

1 cup warmed milk

Serves 2-4

DIRECTIONS:

1. Prepare potatoes for mashing: boil, bake or steam as directed in this chapter. Warm, but don't boil the milk.
2. Hand mash.
3. Blend in warm milk, then add the butter pieces. For thinner or creamier consistency, add more milk.
4. Add salt and pepper to taste. Beat with a fork until fluffy.

MASHED POTATO VARIATIONS

- For a tangy edge, add horseradish or wasabi paste to taste.
- Add shredded Cheddar or parmesan cheese.
- Mix in 1/4 cup crumbled bacon.
- Add any chopped herbs you like, chives, parley, cilantro, basil.
- Lower calorie, use 1/3 cup fat-free chicken or vegetable stock in place of milk.

GARLIC MASHED POTATOES
(My #1 Favorite)

1. Peel off papery covering of 3 garlic cloves.
2. Slice the top off the cloves. Drizzle with oil.
3. Place in a small baking pan or pie tin.
4. Bake 25-30 minutes at 350° or until the cloves are soft. Cool.
5. Prepare manly mashed potatoes as directed above.
6. Squeeze garlic clove and mix into the potatoes before mashing.

OR

1. Chop cloves into small pieces.
2. Sautee in oil or stock until soft.
3. Drain and set aside.
4. Combine with potatoes and mash together.

MAKE-AHEAD POTATO SKINS

1. Bake the potato. Scoop out the pulp from the skin.
2. Mash with 2 teaspoons of milk or melted butter.
3. Put the mixture back into the skin. Wrap in plastic. Refrigerate.
4. When you're ready to reheat, unwrap, put the skins in a baking pan at a 350° oven for 10 minutes, or in a microwave for 2 minutes until it's heated through.
5. Top with one or several of the following: sour cream, herbs, parmesan, bacon bits, your favorite cheese, chili, pizza sauce or salsa. OR create a combination with things you like. It's your potato reality.
6. For health/weight concerns, just use lemon juice or serve with Dijon mustard.

GORDON SAYS: *If you have leftover mashed potatoes, add a teaspoon of lemon juice over the top and refrigerate in a tight-lidded container. To re-heat, put potatoes in a saucepan with a few tablespoons of milk or chicken stock. Stir with medium heat until hot. Add extra butter for more flavor.*

> **"If a fellow really likes potatoes, he must be a pretty decent sort of fellow."**
>
> —A. A. Milne, author, *Winnie the Pooh*

MEAT AND POTATOES

Now that you have the basic starches, I'm going to show you how to roast a variety of meats for your main courses. You can save these in the refrigerator and use in casseroles, breakfast scrambles, or with a side salad or vegetable when you come home from work. Red meat has been demonized as a source of a variety of illnesses but like anything, moderation is the key. Some of those health problems come from a poor diet that is high in fat and low in fiber. Beef has muscle-building protein and B vitamins. A 3-ounce serving has as much iron as three cups of raw spinach; you'd have to eat eleven servings of tuna to get as much zinc. A 3-ounce portion is about the size of a deck of cards. The best kind of meat to buy for a more healthy diet has less fat. Beef is graded for quality by the U.S. Department of Agriculture based on the amount of fat in the meat (marbling). Here are the three grades you see in the store.

Abundant Marbling   Less Marbling   Lean

How much meat should I buy? The amount is determined by several factors. For example, is it boneless, does it have a lot of fat? Bone-in roasts have an average of 2-3 servings while you might get 4-5 servings from one that is just meat. Another thing to consider is who you're feeding. If your girlfriend is coming over for dinner, purchase less than if you're cooking for your poker buddies. Not all chefs agree on the perfect roasting method; put four in a room and you'll have four opinions. I like to "sear" my beef roasts on high, then lower the temperature because this seals in the juices. The best way to tell if meat is done is to get an internal cooking thermometer. It can be used on all types of oven-prepared food including casseroles and egg dishes. Temperature is the best way to tell whether food is cooked sufficiently to kill harmful bacteria like salmonella and e coli. It also takes the guesswork out of knowing when a steak is rare, medium or well done. Cooking thermometers need to be inserted properly. Never position it next to the bone because that conducts heat and will result in a false reading. Insert the stem into the thickest section of meat, away from the bone. Basic gauge thermometers start around $10; digital types can be as high as $50. For $75 you can get a talking remote that tells you when you're food is ready. The probe and digital instant read are not meant to be left in food during cooking. Whichever you choose, be sure that the numbers are easy to read.

Basic Probe

Digital Probe

Digital Wireless

MEAT	Internal Temperatures (approximate)
BEEF	
Boneless roast, tenderloin	Well done: 170°
POULTRY	
Whole chicken / turkey	180°
Poultry-breast	170°
Duck	180°
LAMB	
Leg of lamb, rack of lamb	Rare: 125° Medium Rare: 130° Medium: 140° Medium Well: 150° Well Done: 160°
GROUND MEAT LOAVES	
Beef, veal, pork, turkey, chicken	160°

Oven roasting temperatures may vary depending on your equipment and how old it is. You can get an inexpensive oven thermometer to gauge the temperature. Also remember that cooking times may vary at higher altitudes. For a standard roast, prime rib or rib eye, sear the meat at 400° for 30 minutes, then lower to 325°. You can figure on an average of 13 minutes per pound for a 4-6 pound roast. If you make a roasted meat in advance, you can use the leftovers with rice, pasta or potatoes, or for sandwiches and casseroles. We've covered oven temperatures but you need to know that some beef cuts shouldn't be roasted. The muscles used the most need to be cooked with slow, moist heat: braising, boiling and stewing. Less used, tender muscles use dry heat: roasting, sautéing, broiling and grilling.

GORDON'S TIP: *If you don't have a grill or you live in a place with an Arctic winter, you can cook steaks in the oven or pan fry them.*

OVEN COOKED STEAKS

1. Grease a broiler pan or baking sheet with cooking spray. Aluminum foil is less clean up but I don't like to use it.
2. Adjust oven rack to top position.
3. Brush steaks with olive oil, salt and pepper and place steaks in the pan.
4. Turn oven to broil. Cook 3 to 4 minutes on each side, for rare to medium rare. Add 2 to 3 minutes per side for more well-done meat.
5. Let steak cool 5 minutes before cutting.

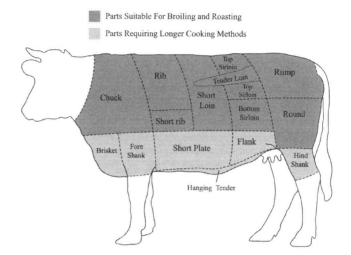

This graphic and the chart below outline the cuts of beef and their preferred cooking methods.

CUTS OF BEEF		
CHUCK	**LOIN**	**RUMP & ROUND**
Chuck 7-Bone Roast	Porterhouse Steak	Skirt Steak
Chuck Pot Roast	T-Bone Steak	Flank Steak
Chuck Steak	Strip Steak	Top Round Steak
Chuck Eye Steak	Filet Mignon	Bottom Round Roast
Flat Iron Steak	Tenderloin Roast	Bottom Round Steak
Shoulder Pot Roast	**SIRLOIN**	Eye Round Roast
Shoulder Steak	Top Sirloin Steak	Eye Round Steak
Ranch Steak	Tri-Tip Steak	Round Tip Roast
Shoulder Petite Tender	Tri-Tip Roast	Round Tip Steak
Short Ribs	**SHANK & BRISKET**	Sirloin Tip Center Roast
RIB	Shank Cross Cut	Sirloin Tip Center Steak
Ribeye Steak	Brisket Flat Cut	Sirloin Tip Side Steak
Rib Roast	**PLATE & FLANK**	Cubed Steak
Ribeye Roast	Skirt Steak	Beef for Stew/ Kabobs
Back Ribs	Flank Steak	**HANGING TENDER**
		Hanger Steak

The last recipe we'll give in this chapter is for a basic comfort food: meatloaf. It's easy to make and with just a few simple substitutions is one of the most versatile dishes you can prepare.

MOUTH WATERING MEATLOAF

1-1/2 pounds ground beef*
(or 1 lb beef and ½ lb ground pork)
3 slices white bread or 1 cup soft breadcrumbs
3/4 cup barbeque sauce
1 medium onion, chopped
1 egg, lightly beaten
2 garlic cloves, minced
1 teaspoon salt
1/4 teaspoon pepper

* Substitute turkey or chicken for less fat content

Serves 4

DIRECTIONS:
1. Preheat oven to 350°.
2. Remove crusts from bread and process slices in a blender or food processor to make crumbs.
3. In a bowl, combine the beef, beaten egg, ½ cup barbeque sauce, breadcrumbs, garlic, onions, salt and pepper. Don't over mix or it could make the meatloaf rubbery.
4. Shape mixture into a loaf about 8" x 5".
5. Place in a 9" x 5" x 3" loaf pan. If you don't have a loaf pan, shape the meat into a loaf and place it on lightly greased cookie sheet. Be sure it has 1" sides to catch the juices.

Spread 1/4 cup barbeque sauce on top.

6. Bake for 1 hour or until internal temperature is 160°. Remove and let stand 10 minutes before slicing.

MEATLOAF VARIATIONS

- Place 6 slices of bacon across the top before baking.
- Add 2 teaspoons Worcestershire sauce or Cajun spices to the mixture.
- Make a hole in the center and stuff with blue cheese. Close loaf & bake.
- Add 1 cup parmesan cheese and substitute tomato sauce or ketchup for barbeque sauce.

Unlike some girlfriends I've had, meatloaf keeps on giving. Can't you just taste those leftover meatloaf sandwiches? This is an Italian makeover of our American staple.

LEFTOVER MEATLOAF PARMIGIANA

1. Place slices, about 1/2" thick, in a baking pan.

2. Spoon leftover marinara sauce or tomato sauce over each slice.

3. Sprinkle shredded mozzarella or place a slice of mozzarella cheese on each piece.

4. Bake in a pre-heated 350° oven for 10 minutes or microwave on high for 2 minutes.

GORDON'S TIP: *Meatloaf can be rock-hard. For a perfect consistency that will get you rave reviews—use soft, not dry breadcrumbs. You can also substitute rolled oats for breadcrumbs!*

Okay. I've given you some of the cooking basics. When you feel comfortable, break out. Break the rules. Be creative. Be innovative. There are hundreds of free websites with recipes you can check out. A few of my favorites are in the Webliography in the back of this book. Make 'Google' your culinary hotline. Go to a kitchen store and ask questions. Remember, the majority of customers are women. Speaking of women, in the next chapter, I'm going to show you how to use food as a tool for romance to woo and win her love.

"Food is symbolic of love when words are inadequate."

—Alan D. Wolfelt, author, educator, inspirational teacher

NOTES:

CHAPTER

RECIPES FOR ROMANCE

3

I've said it before and I'll say it again…cooking is sexy to women. One reason is that food is sensual. It has texture, aroma and flavor which appeals to the senses. Food and sex make a natural pair. When you prepare a meal for a woman it takes her all the way back to cave days when males were the food providers. Neanderthal man felt good when his primitive babe watched him roast a boar that he killed. Later, after he ate the meat and tossed her the bones, they retired to the other side of the campfire for some raw sex. Relationships have come a long way since then, but the modern female will also get primed by a satisfying meal. Hunger is not a turn-on in any era. One thing you don't really have to stress about when cooking for a date is doing things perfectly; her expectations of your skill are probably pretty low. The kitchen is mostly a female domain. Then again, today you'll find some women don't cook at all. Whatever her culinary skill, she'll be flattered by your effort to make a meal for her.

If your date has any inkling to get naughty, cooking is definitely the closer. Most women are flattered by the attention and if you follow my advice, they'll feel as if you've fed their body and their soul. My "sexcess" rate has been pretty good once I get to cook for a woman. In this chapter, I'll share some of my tips and recipes which will help you make out in the kitchen and the bedroom.

> **"After a perfect meal, we are more susceptible to the ecstasy of love than at any other time."**
>
> —Dr. Hans Bazli

MY CULINARY CREED FOR ROMANCE

♥ Don't cook for a woman until you know her food preferences. You can find out a lot dining out on a first date, even at a casual meal. Observe what she orders. Is she a meat eater, on a diet or a vegetarian? Observe how she orders. Does she select something straight from the menu or insist on substitutions, additions and changes that drive the chef crazy? Once you know her food fetishes, you can begin to think about having her over.

♥ Remember, you are bringing a woman into your lair. Be sure it's neat and clean when she walks in. Nothing will turn her off faster than a filthy bathroom with the toilet seat up or a dirty kitchen. Hire a maid if you don't want to do it yourself. Your place could probably use a major cleaning anyway. Hang up your clothes or at least stash them in a closet she isn't likely to open. Recycle those three weeks worth of newspapers, arrange magazines neatly, tidy-up your desk— chaos is not conducive to romance.

♥ Prepare as much as you can in advance. Don't try to shop for everything on the day you're preparing dinner. If you want to pick up some flowers or a loaf of fresh baked bread, that's okay, but go early enough in the day so you don't get frazzled and time crunched. Use my tried and true adage: K.I.S.S., i.e., Keep It Simple and Sensuous. Don't try to get elaborate. Make easy dishes with few ingredients and something that doesn't require intricate preparation or precise timing. Invite her into the kitchen and give her a taste of the delicious things to come. This will start stimulating her senses. Just before she arrives, simmer some garlic and onions in a small amount of stock. This will fill the house with an enticing aroma when she walks in the door. It's all about the senses and smell is a powerful seducer.

♥ Don't venture into ethnic cuisine. Even if you share the same nationality, your version will be up for comparison with her family fare or how she makes the traditional dish. Later on, you can bond in the kitchen swapping ancestral recipes but for that first meal, keep your courses in the culinary mainstream.

♥ Create a romantic space. She should feel peaceful and nurtured. Intimate lighting is essential to creating an amorous atmosphere. Dim the lights. A simple way to create a seductive mood is to put a pastel bulb in your lamp. Get a pair of inexpensive candlesticks and put candles on the table. Make sure it's the drip-free kind. You don't want the distraction of wax all over the table. Put a scented candle in the bathroom. The bedroom is one place you most likely have a wick or two already.

♥ Since ancient Egyptian times, flowers have symbolized love and desire. They show that you put some thought into making the evening special. If you put an arrangement on the table, keep it short so nothing comes between you and her loving gaze while you dine. If you know what her favorite flower is, that's a bonus. Hand her a small bouquet when she arrives for added impact. Maybe you have a flower that has special significance, like one you gave her on your first date. Flowers most often associated with romance are red roses, but others, like daisies, gardenias, lilies, orchids and even wildflowers can set the mood.

♥ If you have a decent table, use some placemats or get an inexpensive cloth to cover any surface stains. If you don't have a dining area, sit on the floor in front of a coffee table or spread a blanket on the floor for a luxurious indoor picnic. Scatter some rose petals on the table or blanket to finish the look. If it's a very special occasion, lay a trail of petals leading to the dining room where you have a table set for dinner. Later in this chapter, I'll show you how to set a table, in case you don't know which side of the plate to put the fork.

♥ Music is a must for a romantic evening whether your date is an executive or a punk rocker. Put on something soft; heavy metal doesn't usually conjure up loving images. A ring tone can be jarring and distracting, so you both need to turn off your cell phones and pagers. Unless one of you is a doctor on call or press secretary to the president, romance should be the sole focus of your attention.

♥ Try to have the kitchen fairly organized before dinner. As for clean up afterwards, see how the evening goes. If you plan things well, you'll just have a few dishes and pots. Only a brain dead guy would not know this: if it looks like you're going to score, don't blow it by cleaning up. Tomorrow is another day. Don't take her up on it if she offers to help!

The bottom line to a really romantic evening is the allure of slowness. Celebrate the food; revel in the sheer pleasure of the tastes and textures that will arouse her senses and her sex.

FACTS ABOUT APHRODISIACS

Aphrodisiacs are foods that are purported to ignite passion and desire. Is it true? Do such foods exist? Do they work? Some experts believe they do. Certain aphrodisiacs are high in amino acids and certain enzymes can increase energy, firing up hormone levels. Several herbs do stimulate nerve centers in the spine which can improve sexual performance. It's just chemistry. One of the most well-known aphrodisiacs is Spanish fly but stay away—it's made from pulverized beetles. Taken internally, it mimics arousal by irritating the urogenital tract and the side effects are not sexy.

Renowned lothario Casanova used oysters to fuel his passion and ate them for breakfast using his lover's breasts as a plate. The mollusks are high in zinc which raises sperm and testosterone production; they also contain dopamine, a hormone that whets the sexual appetite. Oysters are slippery and opening them can be erotic but I don't recommend this unless you know that she likes them or won't be grossed out by downing a living thing.

Some of the recipes in this chapter have aphrodisiac ingredients. Let's take a look at what we eat and how it affects what takes place between the sheets.

♥ **Avocado**: The Aztecs actually called this "fruit from the testicle tree." The B6 and potassium in avocados can stimulate the sex drive, enhancing both male and female libidos. They also have high levels of folic acid which help metabolize protein and give you more energy. During the harvest, Aztec virgins were forbidden to go outside.

♥ **Almonds**: The smell of almonds has been said to excite a woman. Try lighting some almond scented candles before dinner to put her in the mood. These nuts are also a prime source of essential fatty acids which help with production of healthy male hormones. A marzipan (almond paste) heart for dessert will ignite her passion.

♥ **Bananas**: The shape and texture of this fruit can be a suggestive form of foreplay. Aside from the phallic overtone, bananas have B vitamins and potassium which produce sex hormones.

♥ **Celery**: That's right men, rabbit food. She'll think you're being thoughtful about her diet but munch along. It has androsterone, an odorless male hormone released when you sweat to attract the opposite sex. Crushed celery seeds or grated celery root are a tasty addition to a salad and can also turn her on.

♥ **Strawberries and raspberries**: In erotic literature, these are described as "fruit nipples." Drop them in champagne for an enticing cocktail or hand feed each other a luscious strawberry dipped in melted chocolate.

♥ **Fruit**: There's a memorable scene in the film Tom Jones where Mrs. Walters and Tom sit across the table, gazing wantonly, juices dribbling from the fruit they are devouring. When you feel comfortable with each other, hand feed your lover a succulent peach, then kiss the juice from her lips. Slice a peach, papaya or avocado and nibble it into a kiss.

♥ **Figs**: A plump, soft, open fig is a very sexy fruit because it resembles the female sex organ. Break one open and eat it slowly to arouse your woman or feed it to her. Figs are also high in amino acids which improve sexual stamina.

♥ **Chocolate**: It's been said this confection is the surest way to a woman's sweet spot. Some call it a sure-fire aphrodisiac because of PEA, a chemical which is believed to produce the feeling of "being in love." Its effect on the libido got it banned in early monastic sects.

- ♥ **Cheese**: What Casanova didn't know was that cheese contains more PEA than chocolate. Cheese and crackers before dinner or a cheese platter afterwards will get her in the mood.
- ♥ **Shellfish**: Shrimp and lobster are said to feed the brain and fuel the sex drive. Bathe a bite in cocktail sauce or butter. Brush it gently across her lips before she devours the tasty, dipped morsel.
- ♥ **Tomato**: Also called the 'love apple' for its allegedly libido enhancing anti-oxidant, lycopene.
- ♥ **Veggies**. Invigorating ones are peppers, asparagus, carrots, spinach and watercress.

After dinner, too much coffee can depress the sex drive but a small amount can stimulate you both for an "all nighter." Espresso served in small demitasse cups is the perfect compromise. Adding anisette not only sweetens it but also increases desire, so said the Romans who sucked on anise seeds which they believed conveyed special sexual power. If you're still interested in dessert, combine food and fantasy. Dip strawberries, pineapple, bananas, apple slices or lady fingers into warm, melted sweet chocolate. Coat it with whipped cream for an even more exciting experience. Angel food cake with its moist consistency can start juices flowing. Lemon meringue is smooth, sexy and passionate. But it's all American ice cream that can be the most tantric and tantalizing as you find imaginative places to lick it off.

THE MATCH GAME

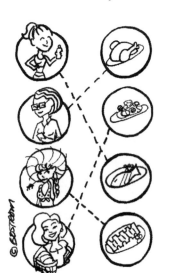

What's the first thing that attracts you to a woman? Usually it's physical first, then you discover her personality. Many a pretty girl has completely ruined the fantasy for me when she revealed her true self. Men's magazines and websites have even categorized types of women you should date, like Miss Sweet, Miss Independent or Miss Loyal, and ones to avoid, like the Gold Digger, Leech or Debater. For me, cooking at home for a date involves more than pop psychology definitions. The recipes I'm going to give you in this chapter will work for almost every type, but let's identify a few and look at some simple ways you can plan your menu. These are quick generalizations for matching foods but will give you some idea of what to serve.

Work-Out Wonder: She sweats hard to keep that shape so don't serve her creamy sauces with buttery mashed potatoes. She's probably counting calories and carbs too. Keep it lean and low-fat for this chick. Go light on the oil in the salad dressings. Poached salmon with a dill sauce accompanied by steamed veggies, a chilled white wine and fruit for dessert are a great menu.

Office Professional: She probably eats salads for lunch to fit into those business suits. After a long day or hard week at work, she needs to relax. Chill the martini glasses and get some of those Roquefort stuffed olives. A sure bet for this type is orange chicken or anything cooked in wine. She's a perfect candidate for those luxurious chocolate-dipped strawberries.

Country Girl: You don't have to be from the South to appreciate down-home fare. She's easy going and outdoorsy, enjoys hiking and camping. You could skip the appetizer and go straight for a hearty meal, like oven barbequed beef short ribs, served with greens, muffins and a fruit cobbler for dessert. Don't forget the beer and the Blake Shelton CD.

Whole Foodie: Think organics and free range. Find out if she's a vegetarian or if she only eats chicken and fish. Some women don't eat dairy. My mushroom walnut paté appetizer has charmed even the most hard-core carnivores. For a main course, you can make pasta with pesto sauce or vegetables (primavera). Ask if she needs gluten- free. For dessert, serve organic chocolate. Strict vegans don't eat anything with a face. Better hope she makes an exception for you!

Park Avenue Princess: This one may be used to fine dining in fancy restaurants but your meal doesn't have to break the bank. Start with raspberries served in Prosecco. Cornish game hens with apricot glaze, asparagus and a nice crème brûlée would be a good menu. Eating these birds can be very erotic. The key to this babe's meal is presentation. Don't slop food on the plate. Garnish with edible flowers or fresh herbs.

The Naughty Princess: She's sexy right out the gate. If you're lucky enough to land one of these women, don't take her for granted. This princess will love that you're preparing a meal just for her. It almost doesn't matter what you cook as long as you remember her food preferences. I'd make something that you can snack on later, like a roast so you can makes sandwiches when you're hungry between bed bouts. The Naughty Princess makes a great food playmate: think whipped cream, fresh fruit juices, honey—you get the picture. If not, you don't deserve that siren.

Neighbor Girl: You don't know what her type is but she could be just your type. You've seen her at the pool, in the laundry room, in the elevator and you want to know her better. You may have even become friends by just hanging out or watching a movie. If you want to take it further, make dinner together. Partnership is very attractive to women. Work to create your own recipes. Talk about food—it's one of the most non-confrontational subjects on the planet. Discussing politics, movies or religion can get you into trouble. I've never had a problem with any woman talking about food. Maybe you have some pasta sauce you've made. Invite her in, toss a salad, throw in some garlic bread and seal the meal with a nice Chianti. Ice cream for dessert will complete this comfortable menu. It's safe to accept her offer to help you clean up. Best friends can make the best lovers.

DINING UNDER THE STARS

This section is not about going outside, but it is far out. How many times have you heard this from a woman, "What's your sign?" Whether you're in California or Kalamazoo, people read their horoscopes in newspapers, magazines, online, and even skeptics sneak a peak at their daily forecast. If you think it's a bunch of hooey that's okay, skip this part,  but most women think otherwise. The point is that the stars are another tool you can use for a romantic evening. Your date will be impressed that you went to the trouble of finding foods in tune with her zodiac. It will demonstrate your incredible sensibility and desire for compatibility. Each sign in the zodiac is associated with one of the four elements: Fire (spirit and energy), Earth (material things and security), Air (intellect and communication) and Water (emotion and nurturing). Here's a quick guide for some foods to help you harmonize with her sun sign. Always remember to consider food preferences and allergies above all.

Aries (Mar 19- April 21), Leo (Jul 23- Aug 22), Sagittarius (Nov 22-Dec 21)

FIRE: These hot women are forthright, self-confident, energetic, generous and impulsive. Cook a hearty meat dish with bold ingredients. Season with garlic, peppers, scallions, mustard, cinnamon, nutmeg. Vegetables that work well are carrots, olives and squash. Fruits that quench their fiery nature are oranges, tangerines, pineapple, watermelon and strawberries. An outrageous fruit tart would be a great dessert.

Taurus (Apr 20-May 21), Virgo(Aug 23-Sep 22), Capricorn (Dec 22-Jan 19)

EARTH: Women ruled by Earth are just that—down-to-earth, good-natured, reliable, loyal and responsible. Food should be tasty and spices subtle for these common sense chicks—basil, dill, bay leaf, parsley. They won't be impressed by exotic delicacies so serve something wholesome like roast chicken with fresh vegetables and a spinach-tomato salad. A fruit cobbler would be a good finish for this earthy meal.

Gemini (May 22-June 20), Libra (Sep 23-Oct 22), Aquarius (Jan 20-Feb 18)

AIR: If you have an air sign over, most likely she's sociable, upbeat, logical and communicative. Don't be afraid to cook something unconventional but not hot and spicy. Anise, fennel, almonds and mint are ingredients that would work. Keep the entrées light and airy too. An eggplant dish or a broiled fish can be accompanied by cauliflower, peas or carrots. Complete your feast with a light, sweet treat like lemon meringue pie or chocolate mousse.

Cancer (June 21–July 22), Scorpio (Oct 23-Nov 21), Pisces (Feb 19-Mar 20)

WATER: Women born under these signs are intuitive, sensitive, spiritual, romantic, supportive and have a good sense of humor. To start, you could serve shrimp cocktail or cucumber salad. Water signs usually eat fish but chicken with mushrooms would be a pleasing entrée for these dreamy mermaids. Pumpkin pie with ice cream or anything chocolate are your best bets for dessert.

THE ART OF THE TABLE

Even though you're eating at home, don't treat this night the same as when you have the guys over. I don't expect you to have fine bone china and a silver service but I'm telling you that plastic forks and paper plates are out. You can get an inexpensive set of dishes and flatware at most chain stores. Check out a restaurant supply because they can have pretty good prices. Even a thrift store would have what you're looking for. You only have to buy for two but I'd get a service for four.

Now, here's what to do with them. You've all eaten out in restaurants but when it comes time to put a fork next to a plate, you may get confused. No wonder. There are settings for formal, informal and casual dinners and the extreme would be a table set for a state dinner at the White House. Setting a table in the U.S. is different from other countries. Traditionally, silverware that is needed first is set to the farthest left and right of the plate. In Europe, the salad fork could be positioned next to the plate because they serve salad after dinner.

Here are two examples of the way you'd set the table for a romantic evening. The first is casual and the second is more formal.

Casual Table Setting

1. Dinner Plate
2. Dinner Napkin
3. Dinner Fork
4. Salad Fork
5. Salad Plate
6. Beverage Glass
7. Dinner Knife (blade faces plate)
8. Teaspoon

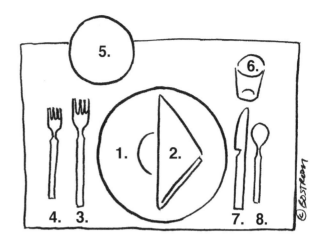

Formal Table Setting

1. Dinner Plate
2. Dinner Napkin
3. Dinner Fork
4. Salad Fork
5. Salad Plate
6. Bread Plate
7. Bread-and-Butter Knife
8. Dessert Fork
9. Water Glass
10. Wine Glass
11. Dinner Knife (blade faces plate)
12. Soup Spoon

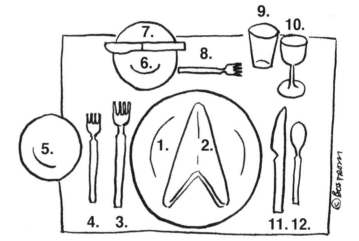

One last word of advice: Don't go crazy over any of this. Whatever you do will be appreciated and unexpected. You can serve her pizza from the box and still make it to home base, but this is about orchestrating a romantic evening.

Now that you have an idea of those basics, I'm going to give you some easy recipes that will make you look like a budding gourmet! This paté will work for meat-eaters and vegetarians alike. Serve it warm on toast triangles or with crackers (not Saltines) and some fine wine.

MUSHROOM & WALNUT PATÉ

INGREDIENTS:

2 tablespoons olive oil

1 lb mushrooms, sliced

1 clove garlic, minced

1 small onion, chopped

1 cup walnuts, chopped *

1/4 lb cream cheese (4 oz.)*

2 eggs

1/4 teaspoon tarragon

Salt & pepper to taste

For a nuttier flavor, add 1/4 cup more nuts.

To lower calories, used reduced fat cream cheese.

DIRECTIONS:

1. Preheat oven to 350°.
2. Coarsely chop walnuts in a food processor or blender.
3. Heat olive oil in a large skillet over medium heat.
4. Sauté walnuts, onions, mushrooms, tarragon and garlic, salt & pepper until veggies are soft.
5. Add the cream cheese and stir until melted. Set aside. Let cool.
6. Put the cooled mixture into a blender or food processor. Add the eggs.
7. Purée or blend until well mixed. Turn into a small baking dish.
8. Bake at 350° for 35 minutes. Let cool when done.
9. Serve on crackers or toast rounds.

GORDON'S TIP: *Put the leftovers in a plastic container. They will keep for a week in the fridge.*

Here's a very elegant, impressive appetizer that has a short prep time and needs no cooking. The mousse mixture can be prepared a day or two in advance.

SHRIMP MOUSSE ON CUCUMBER ROUNDS

INGREDIENTS:

1 cup cooked shrimp *

1/4 pound cream cheese (4 oz.)**

1/4 cup sour cream

A pinch of dill

Salt & Pepper to taste

2 large seedless cucumbers, unpeeled

Substitute salmon for shrimp

**Lower calorie, used reduced fat cream cheese and sour cream*

Makes about 25-30 rounds

DIRECTIONS:

1. Slice cucumbers into 1/8" pieces with skin on.
2. Puree shrimp in a food processor or blender.
3. Add cream cheese and sour cream.
4. Puree well until the texture is smooth and creamy.
5. Chill for 3 hours or overnight.
6. When ready to serve arrange cucumber rounds on a serving platter.

GORDON'S WARNING: *Put the unused mousse in the refrigerator in a plastic or glass container. Do not leave out as it could spoil.*

It's hard to believe how easy this elegant dish is to make and how good it is. Prep is about 10 minutes and in the time it takes to bake, anything can happen.

CORNISH HENS WITH APRICOT GLAZE

INGREDIENTS:

2 Cornish Hens (approx. 1 to 1-1/2 lbs)

1/3 cup chicken stock (or 2 frozen stock cubes)

1/3 cup apricot preserves

Variations:

Brandy Glaze:
Warm 1/2 cup red currant jelly and 1/2 cup brandy in a saucepan.

Apple-Honey Glaze:
1/4 cup honey
2 tablespoons unsweetened apple juice
1 tablespoon lemon juice
1 teaspoon low sodium soy sauce
Mix together

DIRECTIONS:

1. Wash and dry the hens.
2. Combine the honey and apricot preserves in a bowl.
3. Place the hens, skin side up, in a shallow baking pan.
4. Baste with the apricot mixture.
5. Bake at 425° for 30 minutes.
6. Lower temp to 350° and baste again.
7. Continue cooking for 45 minutes or until golden brown or when internal temperature reaches 185°.

Serves 2

Serve with baby carrots tossed with butter and maple syrup, a salad and chilled white wine.

Here's another simple recipe that will make you look like a pro.

ORANGE CHICKEN

INGREDIENTS:

2 plump skinless, boneless chicken breasts

2 tablespoons olive oil

1/2 cup white wine or chicken broth*

1/3 cup orange marmalade

1 cup flour

2 tablespoons of butter

You can use orange juice for a stronger fruit taste

Serves 2

DIRECTIONS:

1. In a skillet, heat the olive oil over a medium flame.
2. While the oil is heating, put the flour in a baking dish and coat each side of the chicken breasts.
3. Sear the floured chicken over high heat, about 1 minute each side.
4. Add 1/4 cup liquid. Cover the pan, turn the heat down to low.
5. After about 5 minutes uncover and check to be sure the liquid is not evaporated. Add more wine, stock or juice if it is dry.
6. Cook another 5 minutes. Remove from pan and set aside.

ORANGE SAUCE

1. Add the orange marmalade to the juices in the pan.
2. Mix it up well. This is called deglazing or a reduction.
3. Add 1/4 cup wine, stock or orange juice. Add the butter and stir it together.
4. Cook off the liquid for 2-3 minutes.
5. Pour the heated sauce over the chicken.

Serve with salad, steamed vegetables, rice pilaf and white wine.

Primavera means "Spring" in Italian. It's best to use seasonal vegetables. Substitute according to what's available.

PASTA PRIMAVERA

INGREDIENTS:

1/2 lb pasta, fusilli or farfalle*

1/4 cup olive oil

1 garlic clove, minced

1/4 teaspoon dried basil or 1/4 cup fresh basil, chopped

1/2 cup cauliflower florets

1/2 cup broccoli florets

1/2 cup asparagus spears cut into 1" pieces

1/2 cup roman tomatoes cut into quarters

1/4 cup fresh grated Romano cheese

1/2 teaspoon salt; pepper to taste

*Corkscrew or bow tie pasta

Serves 2-4

DIRECTIONS:

1. Heat oil in a large skillet. Sauté garlic over medium heat until soft. Be careful not to burn it.
2. Add vegetables and basil. Sauté over high heat until vegetables are crisp and tender. Remove from heat and set aside.
3. Fill a spaghetti pot with water. Bring water to a rolling boil. Add pasta and cook until al dente. (about 8 minutes)
4. Drain and toss pasta with cooked vegetables.
5. Turn into a serving bowl and sprinkle with parmesan cheese.

Serve with a tossed salad with Italian vinaigrette dressing, and red or white wine.

This next recipe is great if you like salmon which many women do because of the Omega 3.

POACHED SALMON IN DILL SAUCE

INGREDIENTS:

2 salmon steaks approx 1" thick

1 tablespoon lemon juice

2 tablespoons butter

1/2 cup champagne or white wine

2 teaspoons chopped chives

1 teaspoon dried or chopped dill

Serves 2

DIRECTIONS:

1. Melt butter in a medium skillet. Mix in lemon juice, wine, chives and pinch of dill.
2. Remove skin from salmon. Add fish to skillet mixture. Cover and simmer on very low heat for 30 minutes. Spoon liquid over salmon a few times during cooking.
3. Remove from pan and place on a platter.
4. Turn heat up high and stir until it reaches consistency of a sauce.
5. DILL SAUCE: This will be reduced down from the liquid in the pan. See Step 4.

Serve with a Caesar Salad and white wine or champagne.

For those who eat pork, the "other white meat," here is a very tasty dish for your tasty girl.

SHERRY-APPLE PORK CHOPS

INGREDIENTS:

2 boneless pork chops approx. 1" thick

2 tablespoons butter

1 medium apple, peeled, cut in small pieces

1 medium onion, chopped

1/2 cup dry sherry cooking wine*

1 tablespoon brown sugar

1/2 teaspoon chopped garlic

Salt & Pepper to taste

Substitute orange juice for wine

For lower calories, use honey instead of brown sugar

Serves 2

DIRECTIONS:

1. In a medium skillet, melt butter over a low flame and cook garlic until soft.
2. Add chops and brown in melted garlic butter.
3. Cover the chops with apples. Add the sherry and sprinkle with brown sugar.
4. Cover the skillet. Simmer over a very low flame for an hour or until tender when pierced with a fork. Turn once.
5. Remove and set aside on a serving plate.
6. When done, if there is no sauce left, add more sherry to the pan juices and reduce it down over very high heat.
7. Spoon over chops.

Serve with applesauce, asparagus and Chardonnay or Chablis.

If your date doesn't have a thing about red meat, she's a great find for male carnivores.

OVEN BARBEQUED BEEF SHORT RIBS

INGREDIENTS:

1-1/2 lbs beef short ribs

2 tablespoons vegetable oil

1/2 cup water

1 teaspoon salt

1/2 cup barbeque sauce

MAKE YOUR OWN BARBEQUE SAUCE:

2 tablespoons butter

1 cup tomato ketchup

1 small onion, chopped fine

1 garlic clove, minced

3 tablespoons Worcestershire sauce

1/2 cup brown sugar

1/4 cup water or chicken stock

1 tablespoon Tabasco (optional)

Serves 2

DIRECTIONS:

BARBEQUE SAUCE:

Melt butter in a saucepan and slowly sauté onions and garlic. Add remaining ingredients. Cook slowly until mixture boils and thickens.

1. Pre-heat oven to 350°*.
2. Trim fat from ribs.
3. Heat oil in a large skillet. Brown ribs over medium heat, turning to cook on both sides.
4. Add water and salt. Cook over lowest heat for 2 to 2 1/2 hours turning occasionally.
5. When tender, remove ribs and let cool. *
6. Dip each rib in BBQ sauce until well coated.
7. Place coated ribs side by side in a baking dish.
8. Bake uncovered for 30 minutes. Turn once.
9. Cool 5-10 minutes. Warm sauce and serve.

Steps 1-5 can be done in advance.

Serve these ribs with an arugala salad, mashed potatoes, and a hearty red wine or beer.

All of the entrées can be accompanied by a Caesar salad which originated in the kitchen of the Hotel César in Tijuana, Mexico. An authentic one can be tricky to make the first time out but try this…it's looks harder than it is. There are also good prepared sauces available.

SIMPLE CAESAR SALAD

INGREDIENTS:

1 head Romaine lettuce

DRESSING:*

3 medium garlic cloves

2 egg yolks

2 teaspoons lemon juice

1/2 tablespoon Dijon or dry mustard

1/2 tablespoon anchovy paste or 2 anchovy fillets (Optional)

1/4 cup extra virgin olive oil

1/4 teaspoon ground black pepper

1/4 teaspoon salt

1/4 grated parmesan cheese

1/2 cup croutons

Dressing will keep about 2 days.

Serves 2

DIRECTIONS:

1. Crack eggs and gently transfer the yolk back and forth between the egg shell to separate it from the white. Be careful to break the egg yolk.**

2. Place garlic cloves, egg yolks and anchovy paste in food processor or blender and process for 1 minute.

3. Add lemon juice, mustard and process for a few seconds.

4. Continue processing. Add oil slowly.

5. Wash and rinse 1 head of Romaine lettuce in a salad spinner.

6. Tear leaves into bite sized pieces and place in a large bowl.

7. Toss lettuce with 1/4 dressing to coat leaves. Add another 1/4 cup dressing or more to taste. Add croutons, parmesan cheese and toss. Serve immediately.

**Kitchen stores sell an inexpensive egg separator tool if this seems too hard.

What would dinner be without dessert? Sweets for your sweetheart…

CHOCOLATE DIPPED STRAWBERRIES

INGREDIENTS:

12 large strawberries, washed & dried

4 oz chocolate (white or dark) chopped

2 tablespoons vegetable oil

Double boiler with hot water

Serves 2

DIRECTIONS:

1. Melt chocolate and shortening in the double boiler*, stirring constantly until the chocolate is melted.

2. Immediately dip each strawberry into the melted chocolate. You can use a toothpick to hold fruit.

3. Let the excess chocolate run off.

4. Place on a wax paper or aluminum foil lined plate.

5. Refrigerate at least 15 minutes or until set.

6. Serve with whipped cream.

If you don't have a double boiler, melt the chocolate in a bowl over a pot of simmering water OR Microwave chocolate in a glass bowl on medium or high power. Stop and stir ever 30 seconds until chocolate is smooth.

FRUIT COBBLER

INGREDIENTS:

4 tablespoons butter

3/4 cup sugar

3/4 cup all purpose flour (pre-sifted)

1 teaspoon baking powder

3/4 cup milk

2 cups fresh fruit*

1 tablespoon brown sugar

Sliced peaches, whole blueberries, blackberries apples, strawberries or in combination. For cherry cobbler, use 2 cups pitted cherries with the juice.

DIRECTIONS:

1. Pre-heat oven to 350°.
2. In a mixing bowl, whisk together the sugar, baking powder and salt. Add milk and continue mixing into a smooth batter.
3. Melt butter and grease an 8" square baking dish.
4. Pour batter into the pan. Arrange fruit over the batter to cover.
5. Sprinkle the brown sugar over the top.
6. Bake 50-60 minutes or until batter browns and fruit bubbles.
7. Let stand. Serve warm with ice cream or whipped cream.

Serves 2

After dessert, you'll find that the best course is yet to come. And in the morning if you score, these breakfasts will seal the cooking deal for you!

STRAWBERRY KISSED FRENCH TOAST

INGREDIENTS:

1/4 cup milk

2 eggs

1/2 teaspoon vanilla extract

1/2 tablespoon maple syrup (or agave)

4 slices whole grain bread

1 tablespoon butter

DIRECTIONS:

1. In a small flat baking dish, whisk the milk, eggs, vanilla and maple syrup.
2. Dip each side of the bread slices in the egg mixture (don't make it too soggy).
3. Heat butter in the skillet (don't burn it).
4. Cook to golden brown, about 2 minutes on each side.
5. Top with Strawberry Kisses.

Serves 2

STRAWBERRY KISSES

INGREDIENTS:

1 pint strawberries, washed, stems removed

1/3 cup sugar

1 teaspoon vanilla

1/4 cup water

Serves 2

DIRECTIONS:

1. Chop the berries into medium pieces.
2. Combine strawberries, sugar, vanilla and water in a saucepan.
3. Cook over low heat for 20 minutes stirring occasionally.
4. Serve hot or cold.

GORDON'S TIP: *For a simple "no cook" topping just combine strawberries, sugar and vanilla in a container and refrigerate overnight. Delicious for pancakes and waffles too!*

A SWEET MORNING QUICHE

INGREDIENTS:

4 eggs

2 cups half & half*

4 oz Swiss cheese, shredded

2 oz mozzarella cheese, shredded

8 teaspoons ground nutmeg

1/4 teaspoon salt

1/4 teaspoon pepper

9" unbaked pie shell (can use the roll out crust or a frozen shell)

For a richer taste, use heavy cream.

Serves 2-4

DIRECTIONS:

1. Preheat oven to 350°.
2. Whisk together the eggs, half & half, salt, pepper and nutmeg.
3. Cover the bottom of the pie shell with the cheeses.
4. Pour egg mixture over the cheese.
5. Bake 35 minutes or until it feels firm in the center.
6. Let cool 15 minutes before serving.

The great thing about quiche recipes is there are so many variations. You can add cooked mushrooms, broccoli, onions, bacon, ham, asparagus…get creative with your cooking! To doubly impress your date, use these flaky crescent rolls for a variety of breakfast options. This one is filled with eggs, ham and cheese. You can also fill them with jam for a cool continental breakfast or to accompany the quiche.

CHEESY HAM AND EGG CRESCENTS

INGREDIENTS:

8 refrigerator crescent rolls

7 eggs, cooked and scrambled*

1 cup cooked ham, chopped

1 cup shredded Swiss cheese

Follow directions from Sexy Scramble recipe below

Variations: Add one or more of these to the eggs: Mushrooms, Bacon, Veggies, Cooked onions

Serves 8

DIRECTIONS:

1. Carefully unroll crescents onto a large ungreased cookie sheet.
2. On the wide end of each roll, place a tablespoon of eggs, a teaspoon of ham and top with cheese.
3. Roll up each crescent, starting at the wide end and ending at the narrow end of the crescent.
4. Bake at 375° for 11-13 minutes, or until crescents are golden.
5. Remove carefully with a spatula and serve warm.

SEXY SCRAMBLE

INGREDIENTS:

4 eggs

1/4 Cup milk

1/4 Teaspoon salt

1/4 teaspoon pepper

2 teaspoons butter

Additions: shredded cheese, leftover chopped veggies, crumbled bacon or sausage

Serves 2

DIRECTIONS:

1. Whisk together eggs, milk, salt and pepper.
2. Heat butter in a nonstick skillet, medium heat.
3. Pour in egg mixture with added ingredients.
4. Pull eggs from the side forming large pieces until no liquid remains.
5. Serve immediately with toast or croissants.

Finally, here is a refreshing way to toast to your successful romantic adventure!

PERFECT PEACH BELLINI

INGREDIENTS:

2 cup sliced peaches

1/2 cup water

1 teaspoon lemon juice

1 teaspoon sugar

1 bottle of chilled Prosecco, champagne or dry sparkling wine

Serves 2

DIRECTIONS:

1. Purée peaches, water, lemon juice and sugar in a blender until smooth.
2. Fill a champagne flute a quarter full of the purée.
3. Slowly fill the glass with the Prosecco, champagne or sparkling wine.

I'll close this chapter with a concept I'd like to revive… chivalry. I don't mean putting your raincoat down over a puddle or jousting to defend a lady's honor. Basically, it's a return to common courtesy. Our technology can distance us from physical interaction and sometimes politeness gets lost in the texting. Chivalry is actually a pretty cool concept from the medieval knights of old. There's a whole code of conduct but here are the parts I try to live by:

♥ **Always speak the truth**

♥ **Protect the weak and defenseless**

♥ **Persevere to the end in any enterprise begun**

♥ **Respect the honor of women**

That last one is key to romance. The pendulum has swung to center and women today, even feminists, no longer feel it's an insult to open a door for them or feel protected by a man. And I don't feel any less masculine, if a woman opens the door for me or offers to split the check.

Okay guys. I've armed you with all you need to go from first base to a World Series ring. Play ball!

NOTES:

CHAPTER

EAT WELL
WEIGH LESS

4

Diets. No carb, low carb, no fat, all meat, meatless, grapefruit, rice, fruit…so many choices, so little time to figure it all out. Women know their body types, keep meticulous track of every ounce gained or lost but pounds can creep up on men. When they have to lose weight, men treat it like a military action, often becoming workout fanatics. But without changing what you eat, that fat just turns to muscle. It's also important to understand that men have their own eating habits, patterns and cravings. Not too long ago, a macho man wouldn't eat salad because it was considered feminine. Even today some men won't order it as a main course but consider salad a 'starter.' Men want real food like meat and potatoes, not leaves. No surprise. Men were the hunters. There were no vegetable gardens in the cave yard. Men have dismissed other food as "chick cuisine"—cottage cheese, yogurt, rice cakes, vegetable chips and anything that says low fat. While more men today are savvy about what's good for them, they still have a hard time resisting foods they've been weaned on, like steak, chips and fries. These comfort foods can trigger a man's appetite. How do you control it? Change what you eat and how your body uses it. Also, how your food is prepared is important. This is where I come in.

Let's not talk about diet. Men hate diets, diet food, diet programs, diet portions and dieting, period. Men hate being told what to do. I won't do that. Instead, we'll look at some factors that affect weight. First, we'll look at the way your body burns or metabolizes food. Researchers at Harvard Medical School found that humans tend to eat the same amount of food, no matter what the calories. Equal portions of fat and protein will fill you up and satisfy your hunger; the difference is in the calorie load. Fat, at nine calories per gram, is the densest form of food energy we consume. It's easy to over-indulge in fat not only because it's filling but because it stores quicker and satisfies you faster. Storing 100 calories of protein requires almost twice as much energy as storing 100 calories of fat.

Drastically cutting calories is a bad way to lose weight, so is starving yourself. The body panics. It doesn't know when it's going to get food and switches your calorie burning mechanism to a slower mode which actually stores fat. The trick is to drop calories a little at a time. Today, men eat 200 calories more food energy per day than they did ten years ago; that alone can add 20 pounds annually to your weight. So, it's no surprise that two-thirds of men are overweight. Body Mass Index (BMI), a reliable indicator of body fat, is calculated from your weight and height. Since men are not usually mathematically challenged, you'll have no trouble figuring out yours. Here's the formula: 1.) multiply your weight in pounds by 704.5[1] 2.) divide the result by your height in inches 3.) divide that result by your height in

---

1. This multiplier 704.5 is used by the National Institutes of Health. Other organizations may use slightly different numbers.

inches again. If you don't like math, this is a cool online calculator: www.healthcalculators.org/calculators/bmi.asp

Here is the BMI guideline according to the National Institute of Health.

Underweight	**BMI Less than 18.5**
Normal weight	**BMI between 18.5 – 24.9**
Overweight	**BMI between 25 – 29.9**
Obesity	**BMI of 30 or greater**

Men in the upper end of the "normal" range, who have a BMI between 22 to 24, would generally live longer if they lost some fat. If you use BMI as a measurement tool, you should know that very muscular people may fall into the "overweight" category when they are actually healthy and fit. Let your body be your guide.

How your body burns calories is called metabolism. Why can some men eat whatever they want and others gain weight at the smell of a Big Mac? The answer is your metabolism rate. It speeds up on exertion and burns calories but even at rest you're burning some calories. Picture your body as an engine with a fixed idling speed. The Basal Metabolism Rate (BMR) is the number calories you need to maintain normal body functions. The higher the BMR the faster you burn calories. Physical activity can account for 10% to 30% of calories burned daily, while BMR takes up 70% or more. Since BMR increases with lean body mass, activities that build and tone muscle will burn more calories. Here's an easy BMR calculator: www.calculator.net/bmr-calculator.html

Some researchers debunk the old theory that after age thirty-five your metabolism naturally slow downs and you automatically gain weight. Besides overeating, much of today's weight gain is attributed to inactivity. This is a topic where males also shift into manly gear. They feel like they have to run a marathon, bench press a car, walk the treadmill from New York to L.A. or join a boot camp. Forget that—just start moving. Try ten minutes a day of any kind of movement just three times a week and increase it when you're ready. Work up to an hour. It's a good start to keeping you healthy. Sports are a great way to have fun and burn calories but if you have limited time or mobility, there are some simple things you can do. 1.) Park your car in the farthest spot instead of wasting expensive gas circling the lot to find a closer space. 2.) Take the stairs instead of an escalator or an elevator. 3.) Walk the dog. 4.) Stroll around a museum. 5.) Get off the couch. 6.) Do some sit-ups while you're watching TV instead of making your only exercise reaching for a beer. 7.) Buy a treadmill or a stationary bike online or at a thrift store. My problem is getting motivated but once I start to look and feel better, it's worth it. So, push away from the table and get on your feet.

My favorite *Save the Males* way to burn calories—make love, it's the most enjoyable exercise of all. Remember, the key is fat burn. Exercise speeds up metabolism. As men age they burn fewer calories per pound of body weight because their lean body mass is less. Some researchers think this reduction is solely responsible for metabolism slowdown. You need some exercise. Don't let anyone tell you that you can't increase your muscle size and strength as you get older. The U.S. Department of Agriculture's Human Nutrition Center on Aging at Tufts University found that the muscles of older men are just as responsive to weight training as those of younger ones. Developing an old muscle is just like developing a young muscle. You may need to be more careful and progress slower, but you can do it. Make the decision. That's all there is to it.

TO CARB OR NOT TO CARB

What about the new low-carb craze? Cutting out all carbohydrates and starches is not the answer because they provide the body's main source of ready-to-use fuel. There are good carbs and bad ones. The problem is when you confuse food that has high carbs and high fat ingredients (like muffins or potatoes.) When you consume carbs, your body converts them from starches to sugar molecules which are either burned or stored. Bad carbs break down and are converted quickly to raise your blood sugar. There's a surge of insulin which causes sugar to be stored in muscle and fat. The body hormone that's supposed to signal the body to burn fuel is inhibited. Your blood sugar decreases and then you're hungry again. Low-carb diets work because they force you to cut out 'empty calories' like potato chips, pretzels, candy, refined sugar products and convenience foods we can eat on the run. But remember that low carb is not necessarily low calorie. Carb counting is not dieting. Many products have lower carb counts because they replace sugars with artificial sweeteners and wheat flour with soy flower. That doesn't mean you can eat huge portions of low-carb pasta or bread. One important thing to know is that if your body is completely carb deprived, it can lead to a buildup of partially broken down fats (ketones). This can produce high levels of uric acid, especially bad for kidney problems and diabetes.

A quick male fix for hunger is carbonated drinks. For some men, bubbly beverages have become a favorite breakfast. Soda does provide energy and quells sugar craving. What you don't know is that each additional daily serving of a sugar-sweetened drink multiplies the risk of obesity by 1.6%. Some men say they compensate by eating less but when calories come in liquid form, it shocks the body. A meal has to go through your gut so the brain gets signals that slow your hunger down, but you can drink a 12-ounce soft drink before your body knows what hit it. Depending on the soda, a 12-ounce can has 9-13 teaspoons of sugar! We are not adapted to handle fast-acting carbohydrates.

Let's repeat this from an expert. "Consumers think carb-free is calorie-free, which it's not," says Leslie Bonci, a spokeswoman for the American Dietetic Association (ADA). "They think someone's giving them permission to eat and what's going to happen is, we're going to see people start to gain weight." Remember counting calories does count. So, why even bother cutting carbs? Because if you eat bad carbs, i.e., foods with lots of added sugar and refined starches, you need more to fill you up and you'll get hungry sooner. Whole food, fiber-filled starches (oatmeal, vegetables, beans) are digested more slowly, so you feel full. Here is my advice for your healthiest low-carb approach: eat whole-grain carbs (instead of those made with white flour and lots of sugar) and eat a diet rich in lean meats and veggies. I guarantee you won't starve!

THE GREAT GLUTEN CONTROVERSY

Groceries and health food stores are exploding with gluten-free products from bread to beer. Some restaurants even offer gluten-free choices. That's good news for the 1% of the population with celiac disease, which stems from the inability to digest gluten, the defining protein of wheat, barley and rye. It provides strength and elasticity which is why you can knead bread, roll thin pastry and create the perfect croissant. Celebrities and sports figures have touted the benefits of going gluten-free claiming it's healthier and can help with weight loss. So what's the truth about gluten? The market-research firm Packaged Facts survey showed that only 8% to 12% of people who purchased gluten-free products did so because of gluten intolerance. Time magazine found that most people go gluten-free for the wrong reasons. Almost 50% of people asked thought that gluten-free meant healthier, and 30% bought gluten-free foods to manage their weight. However, gluten free is not a synonym for low carb; the carbs in gluten-free cookies and bagels are still there. Remember what I said before….low carb does not mean low calorie which is the real key to losing weight. Unless people are very careful, a gluten-free diet can lack vitamins, minerals and fiber according to Dr. Peter Green, director of the Celiac Disease Center at Columbia University.[2] All that said, cutting out gluten for those without celiac disease may still have some positive effect. If you stop eating pizza, cake, cookies and replace them with unprocessed alternatives like lean meat, fruit and veggies, you'll probably feel better 'cause you're eating healthy!

CRACKING LABEL CODES

When you're trying to lose weight it's good to read labels. The claims can get confusing—fat-free, light, lean—what does it all mean? What's the truth about serving size, cholesterol, saturated, trans or unsaturated fat? In 1906, the Pure Food and Drug Act was passed to regulate food safety by listing ten 'dangerous ingredients' including opium, cocaine, cannabis and alcohol.

---

[2]. *Bad-Mouthing Gluten*, Katy Steinmetz Monday, May 23, 2011

Fast forward to 1994. The FDA launched labels which actually make claims more accurate and added nutrition information which makes healthy eating easier. Now let's crack the food label code.

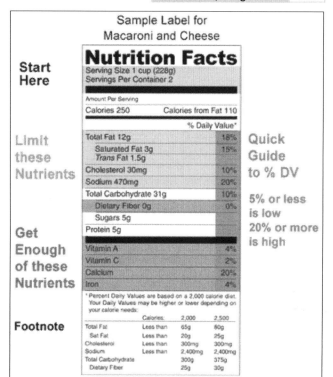

Reduced Fat: 25% less fat than the same regular brand.

Light: 50% less fat than the regular version.

Low-Fat: contains 3 grams or less of total fat.

Low-Calorie: contains 40 calories or less.

Free: one serving contains none, or only a trace amount of whatever it's free of—fat, calories, sodium, cholesterol, sugar.

Lean: contains less than 10 grams of total fat, 4 grams of unsaturated fat and less than 95 milligrams of cholesterol per serving.

Extra Lean: contains less than 5 grams of total fat, 2 grams of unsaturated fat and less than 95 milligrams of cholesterol per serving.

Low Cholesterol: less than 20 milligrams.

Low Sodium: less than 140 milligrams.

Very Low Sodium: less than 35 milligrams.

Good Source of: provides at least 10% of the Daily Value of a particular vitamin or nutrient per serving.

High In: provides 20% or more of the daily value of a specified nutrient per serving.

The last two relate to health claims that the Federal Food and Drug Administration (FDA) allowed manufacturers to use in labeling and advertising. This helps consumers identify foods rich in nutrients that could help prevent chronic disease conditions, such as using low-sodium products to reduce hypertension, calcium-enriched food to help prevent osteoporosis and low-fat cuisine which could reduce the risk of heart disease. Refer to the sample label from the FDA Website.

It's important to check the serving size on the label. The official purpose is two-fold: it tells the amount a person needs to eat to get the listed nutrients and the number of servings in the whole package. The hidden danger is in the number of calories. I looked at a muffin wrapper that listed 240 calories per serving, but one serving was only half a muffin! Not many people would realize that eating a whole muffin means you're consuming 480 calories. They can really add up so be very aware of the actual calorie count.

Men tend to eat more meat which is high in protein but can have lots of fat. Choose a lean cut. Look for loin and round cuts. 'Prime' has higher fat than 'Choice.' For pork, lamb and veal, get the loin or leg. No matter what grade you buy, trim off the fat. Don't be fooled by turkey or chicken substitutes in hot dogs or lunch meats, since they still can be high in fat. Here's are the recommended guidelines for an approximate fat intake for the average active man.

Normal Weight: 80-90 grams – consume 2,500 calories a day

To Lose Weight: 60-70 grams – consume 2,000 calories a day

Another good way to calculate losing weight is this: if you want to take off one pound per week, reduce calories by 500 per day. Try eating 250 calories less per day and exercising enough to burn 250 calories. The easiest way to cut back on calories is to watch your portion sizes. Remember, this caloric intake will vary with height and weight but the bottom line is that to lose weight you have to cut down fat and burn more calories than you consume. To find the recommended number of calories per day for your activity level, check out: www.freedieting.com/tools/calorie_calculator.htm. To calculate the amount of fat intake try this online calculator: www.healthcalculators.org/calculators/fat.asp

CHOLESTEROL, FAT AND FICTION

You got that dreaded doctor's report...your cholesterol is too high. Yikes. How did that happen? First, let's look at what it is and how it works in the body. Cholesterol is a soft, waxy substance found in all of your body's cells. It's used for producing membrane and hormones, among other functions. Your body actually makes cholesterol which is why some people have naturally higher levels. Cholesterol and other fats can't dissolve in the blood but need carriers called lipoproteins. Low-density lipoproteins (LDL) are bad because they transport cholesterol from the liver to your tissues and body cells. Too much LDL clogs the arteries and together with other substances form plaque, increasing the risk of heart attack and stroke. When we eat fatty foods, we raise the bad LDL cholesterol in the bloodstream. The body also produces "good" cholesterol, high-density lipoproteins (HDL) which carries unused cholesterol from the tissues to the liver where it's broken down and disposed of. Some experts believe that high levels of HDL may even reduce the risk of heart disease. Remember, high cholesterol has no symptoms. The only way to find out if you're in the danger zone is to get a blood test.

Let's look at the relationship between fat and cholesterol. Everyone needs a certain amount of fat in a healthy diet because it helps lubricate joints and is used for energy. One fat gram has 9 calories. Keep that in mind when you're reading labels. Fat in the food we eat falls into two basic types: saturated and unsaturated. Saturated fats come from animal products like meat and dairy, or from tropical oils like coconut or palm. Talking about fat is important because the type you eat can affect your cholesterol level. There are bad fats (saturated), good fats (unsaturated) and a new nefarious trans-fatty acid. When it was discovered that saturated fats raised cholesterol levels, the food industry couldn't switch to unsaturated fats because they got rancid too quickly. They solved the problem by forcing hydrogen gas at a high temperature and pressure into vegetable oils. This created trans-fatty acids which not only increase the bad LDL, they decrease the good HDL. Oil is 100% fat and total hydrogenation would make them too solid which is why you see the term partially-hydrogenated. The worst offender is margarine but most processed, fried foods and even baked goods have trans fats. You think a bran muffin is better for you, right? If it's made with partially hydrogenated vegetable oil, it's not. Start checking labels and you'll be shocked at how many contain trans-fatty acids. I like olive oil and I am a big fan of coconut oil.

GORDON'S WARNING: *If the fat has been eliminated or cut back, the amount of sugar in the food may have increased, adding calories.*

We discussed eating lean red meat. When the label says "lean" that means the cut has less than 10 grams of total fat, 4.5 grams or less of saturated fat and less than 95 milligrams or less of cholesterol per 3.5-ounce serving. Look for "loin" or "round." The charts in the Appendix are great guidelines for the fat and nutrients in the leanest cuts of beef.[3] If you want to further reduce fat in your diet, chicken is a good bet. The leanest part is the breast. Remember to remove the skin before cooking since keeping it on doubles the amount of fat, or you can leave the skin on to keep it juicy and don't eat it, no matter how crispy! When selecting a cut of pork, look for "choice" or "lean". Roasted and broiled chops and loins with a bone tend to have slightly more cholesterol. Let's compare the nutrition in a 3.5 ounce (100 grams) serving of each: roasted, skinless chicken breast, broiled T-bone steak, choice grade, trimmed to 1/4" fat and roasted boneless pork loin.

GORDON'S TIP: *Remember, to cut across the grain, find the faint lines running through the beef and cut across the length of these lines, not in the same direction.*

---

3. Charts courtesy of The Beef Checkoff www.BeefItsWhatsForDinner.com

SLOW ROASTED PORK LOIN

INGREDIENTS:

3 lbs lean pork loin

1-1/2 cups apple cider

1/3 cup maple syrup (pure) or agave

3 tablespoons Dijon mustard

1/2 teaspoon salt

1/2 teaspoon black pepper, coarse grind

1 tablespoon vegetable oil

1 lb fingerling potatoes

1 medium onion, peeled and cut into wedges

6 medium carrots, peeled and cut into 2" pieces

2 medium fresh apples, cut into 1" pieces

Serves 6-8

TO MAKE THE SAUCE:

After the pork and veggies are removed from baking dish, strain the liquid into skillet. Add apples and cook over medium heat until apples are soft, about 4-5 minutes.

Remove apples and cook down the sauce 3 minutes or until thickened. .

DIRECTIONS:

1. Preheat oven to 350°.
2. Whisk together cider, syrup and mustard in a small bowl.
3. Season pork with salt and pepper. Cook in a skillet over medium heat, turning until browned on all sides about 4-5 minutes.
4. Remove from heat. Set aside. Add cider mixture to the skillet and cook 1-2 minutes.
5. Place carrots and onions on the bottom of the baking dish. Put the browned pork on top.
6. Arrange potatoes around the roast. Pour cider mixture over it.
7. Bake, covered* 40-45 minutes. (internal temperature of pork is 145° F.)
8. Remove from oven. Place pork on a cutting board. Let stand 10 minutes before slicing. Move potatoes and carrots to a serving platter.
9. Slice pork and serve on the platter with potatoes, carrots and apples. Serve with sauce.

If you don't have a covered baking dish, you can put foil over it.

CLAY POT METHOD:

1. Soak clay pot top and bottom in cold water for 15 minutes.
2. Follow directions 1-7. Place pot in a cold oven and cook at 425° for 1-1/2 hours. Remove the top and cook for an additional 15 minutes to brown.
3. Let stand 15 minutes before slicing.

Compare the following nutrition labels.

Choice T-Bone Steak

Nutrition Facts
Serving Size 1 T-Bone Steak (100g)

Amount Per Serving
Calories 205 — Calories from Fat 91

	% Daily Values*
Total Fat 10g	15%
Saturated Fat 4g	20%
Trans Fat 0g	
Cholesterol 59mg	20%
Sodium 77mg	3%
Total Carbohydrate 0g	0%
Dietary Fiber 0g	0%
Sugars 0g	
Protein 27g	54%

*Percent Daily Values are based on a 2,000 calorie diet.

Chicken Breast

Nutrition Facts
Serving Size 1 Chicken Breast (100g)

Amount Per Serving
Calories 173 — Calories from Fat 41

	% Daily Values*
Total Fat 5g	8%
Saturated Fat 1g	5%
Trans Fat 0g	
Cholesterol 85mg	28%
Sodium 77mg	3%
Total Carbohydrate 0g	0%
Dietary Fiber 0g	0%
Sugars 0g	
Protein 31g	62%

*Percent Daily Values are based on a 2,000 calorie diet.

Pork Loin

Nutrition Facts
Serving Size 1 Pork Loin (100g)

Amount Per Serving
Calories 252 — Calories from Fat 137

	% Daily Values*
Total Fat 15g	23%
Saturated Fat 5g	25%
Trans Fat 0g	
Cholesterol 81mg	27%
Sodium 48mg	2%
Total Carbohydrate 0g	0%
Dietary Fiber 0g	0%
Sugars 0g	
Protein 27g	54%

*Percent Daily Values are based on a 2,000 calorie diet.

Chicken wins the weight race. It's high in protein and lower in fat, even though it has slightly higher cholesterol. Surprisingly, pork is also a good bet. Here's a great recipe for a roasted pork loin. Use a slow-cooker or clay pot and you'll cut the meat with a fork. Great leftovers for pulled pork tacos or sandwiches!

You can check out more meat and nutrient facts at www.nutritiondata.com, a free, very comprehensive site with a ton of valuable information including a section where you can calculate the nutrition of your own recipes. They also list nutrition facts for nearly every fast food chain menu. Here are the fast fat facts on what you get in a McDonald's Big Mac and a large order of fries.

Big Mac

Nutrition Facts
Serving Size 1 Big Mac (216g)

Amount Per Serving
Calories 590 — Calories from Fat 310

	% Daily Values*
Total Fat 34g	52%
Saturated Fat 11g	55%
Trans Fat 0g	
Cholesterol 85mg	28%
Sodium 1070mg	45%
Total Carbohydrate 47g	16%
Dietary Fiber 3g	12%
Sugars 8g	
Protein 24g	48%

*Percent Daily Values are based on a 2,000 calorie diet.

Large Fries

Nutrition Facts
Serving Size 1 Large Fries (176g)

Amount Per Serving
Calories 542 — Calories from Fat 231

	% Daily Values*
Total Fat 26g	40%
Saturated Fat 4g	20%
Trans Fat 0g	
Sodium 347mg	14%
Total Carbohydrate 68g	23%
Dietary Fiber 3g	12%
Sugars 0g	
Protein 8g	16%

*Percent Daily Values are based on a 2,000 calorie diet.

This lean beef stir fry recipe can be made with chicken or pork too. I recommend farm-raised pork or organic beef.

LEAN BEEF & BROCCOLI STIR FRY

INGREDIENTS:

- 1 lb lean, trimmed sirloin beef, sliced thin, across the grain
- 2-1/2 tablespoons corn starch
- 1/4 teaspoon salt
- 1 cup reduced-sodium chicken broth
- 3 cups broccoli florets
- 3 tablespoons vegetable oil
- 3 medium garlic cloves, minced
- 1 tablespoon fresh ginger, peeled, minced
- 6 green onions chopped
- 1/4 cup low sodium soy sauce
- 1/4 cup water

Serves 6

DIRECTIONS:

1. Mix the salt and 2 tablespoons of corn starch. Coat the beef slices.
2. Heat the oil in a medium-high skillet. Cook beef until lightly browned, 4-5 minutes.
3. Remove with a slotted spoon and set aside.
4. Add 1/2 cup broth and broccoli. Cook, tossing occasionally until tender, about 3 minutes.
5. Add ginger, garlic and green onions and stir fry about 1-2 minutes.
6. Whisk the water, soy sauce and 1/2 tablespoon corn starch until well blended. Add this liquid to the pan.
7. Reduce heat to medium and cook until slightly thickened. Add beef and toss with broccoli.
8. Serve with white or brown rice.

My recommendation if you really want to lose weight is stay away from fast food. The movie *Super Size Me* was a great, irreverent look at America's obesity problem in relation to fast food consumption. Writer/director, Morgan Spurlock tested his body's endurance by eating McDonald's food at every meal for three months. Spurlock gained 20 pounds in 30 days.

It's no wonder. According to McDonald's own nutrition chart, a Big Mac, large order of fries, 16-ounce vanilla shake and apple pie are over 2,000 calories.[4] A 32-ounce shake alone can have as much as 1,110 calories. Spurlock also endangered his body functions. Not surprisingly, his liver was overworked from processing so much fat. I understand that sometimes you're in a bind or a time crunch and you want something fast. The good news is that McDonald's and most every other big chain is responding to heart health and weight issues. Order grilled or broiled meat; be on guard when ordering salads. Lettuce is good but the dressing may have lots of fat. Ask if they have a fat-free or a reduced calorie variety. Tell them you want light mayonnaise on your sandwiches. Check the chain's website nutrition chart which will give you details for each menu item they serve; ask a server where it's posted in the store.

No discussion of weight would be complete without mention of fish. I'm not going to go into all the scientific reports about why fish is good for you. I'll boil it down to one thing: Omega-3 fatty acids. These are good poly-unsaturated fats and have been found to have anti-inflammatory properties, also found in plant-based foods and oils. These good fats are natural blood thinners which can protect against blood clots that can cause heart attacks, and can help stabilize an irregular heartbeat. Scientists studying Eskimos whose diet had lots of salmon, made the connection between a low incidence of heart disease, diabetes, arthritis and other disease, and a high consumption of foods rich in Omega-3 fatty acids. Brain health benefits since there is a link between depression and low concentrations of Omega-3. Here's a nutrition comparison of 3.5-ounce servings of pink salmon, shrimp and canned tuna.

---

4. McDonald's USA Nutrition Facts chart for Popular menu items

Pink Salmon, Cooked

Nutrition Facts
Serving Size (100g)

Amount Per Serving	
Calories 128	Calories from Fat 27
	% Daily Values*
Total Fat 3g	5%
Saturated Fat 1g	5%
Trans Fat 0g	
Cholesterol 42mg	14%
Sodium 377mg	16%
Total Carbohydrate 0g	0%
Dietary Fiber 0g	0%
Sugars 0g	
Protein 24g	48%

*Percent Daily Values are based on a 2,000 calorie diet.

Uncooked Shrimp

Nutrition Facts
Serving Size (100g)

Amount Per Serving	
Calories 106	Calories from Fat 16
	% Daily Values*
Total Fat 2g	3%
Saturated Fat 0g	0%
Trans Fat 0g	
Cholesterol 152mg	51%
Sodium 148mg	6%
Total Carbohydrate 1g	0%
Dietary Fiber 0g	0%
Sugars 0g	
Protein 20g	40%

*Percent Daily Values are based on a 2,000 calorie diet.

White Tuna (water)

Nutrition Facts
Serving Size (100g)

Amount Per Serving	
Calories 220	Calories from Fat 46
	% Daily Values*
Total Fat 5g	8%
Saturated Fat 1g	5%
Trans Fat 0g	
Cholesterol 72mg	24%
Sodium 648mg	27%
Total Carbohydrate 0g	0%
Dietary Fiber 0g	0%
Sugars 0g	
Protein 41g	82%

*Percent Daily Values are based on a 2,000 calorie diet.

I'm a native Californian and wherever I have cooked, everyone loves fish tacos. Most recipes batter and fry the fish. This one is great because it's both tasty and low calorie.

FISH TACOS

INGREDIENTS:

1 lb cod or halibut or any other firm white fish fillet (fresh or frozen)

8 corn tortillas

1 teaspoon cumin

1 teaspoon olive oil

2 tablespoons lime juice

2 tablespoons fresh cilantro, chopped

GARNISHES:

Shredded cabbage

Low fat sour cream

Salsa

Cilantro

Serves 4

DIRECTIONS:

1. Mix the lime juice, olive oil, cumin and cilantro in a small bowl. Place fish in a sealable plastic bag. Add marinade and refrigerate for 15 minutes.

2. Preheat oven to 350°.

3. Coat a baking sheet with cooking spray. Place marinated fish on the baking sheet.

4. Bake for 15-20 minutes, until fish flakes easily with a fork. You can also broil or grill fish, allowing 10 minutes per inch of thickness.

5. Warm tortillas in the oven.

6. Cut the cooked fish into chunks and divide among corn tortillas.

7. Garnish and serve.

MY TIPS FOR KEEPING WEIGHT DOWN

I will now share with you some of my personal tips for keeping your weight down. Don't skip breakfast. You're rushing off to work and trying to beat traffic. Who has time for food? You do. Studies show that skipping breakfast might actually lead to weight gain.[5] It makes sense to eat earlier in the day when you're active and can use the food as fuel for energy. Researchers also found that the bad HDL cholesterol was lower in the subjects who ate breakfast. One doctor I know recommends eating protein in the morning; it boosts metabolism since your body requires more energy to digest protein. It also burns fat which helps preserve and build lean muscle tissue. There's a lot of talk about not eating late at night because you can't burn off the calories. Here's the reality. A calorie is a calorie. Too many will make you gain weight. There's no magic hour at which the body stops burning fat. Your metabolism works even when you're asleep. You can eat the same number of calories at 6 p.m. or 8 p.m. The key is how many you consume. The reason why people lose weight when they don't eat late is usually because they don't eat anything at all. They are cutting calories. The real key is not what time you eat but what you eat at night. You come in from work late and you're starving. You grab the first thing you see to quench that hunger. So, the bottom line is, if you're eating late, even if you're eating out, make healthy food choices.

> **"My doctor told me to stop having intimate dinners for four, unless there are three other people."**
>
> —Orson Welles, American actor

---

5. *American Journal of Clinical Nutrition*, February 2005 vol. 81 no. 2 388-396

Belly up to the bar is not an expression without meaning. Men tend to store fat in the belly. Alcohol has lots of liquid calories which add weight, but a key factor is how the alcohol is used by the body. When the liver coverts it to acetate, it's released into the bloodstream. Since it can't be stored in the body, acetate replaces fat as a source of fuel instead of burning stored fat.

Another way I'm trying to save us males is to remind you that alcohol cuts testosterone levels for up to 24 hours and raises the level of cortisol which affects muscle building. If you're trying to look like Mr. Universe, a barbell is better than a bar stool. I'm not telling you to get on the wagon. You can still lose weight and be virile but drink in moderation. If one beer has 145 calories, downing a six-pack is like eating a whole meal. The solution is not only watching how many drinks you have, but to also watch what you eat with it. Another thing to keep on mind is that drinks with soda or mixes contain a lot of sugar which adds more calories.

I repeat—calories are the key.

Here's a quick chart to give you an idea of what's in the most common drinks. The calories are approximate and may vary with brand.

Drink	Calories
80 proof alcohol -1 oz	80
Wine - 5 oz. glass	100-110
Beer, 12 oz regular	145
Beer, light	105
Beer, lager	120
Beer, strong	180
Beer, stout	190
Scotch – 1 oz	65
Mai Tai – 4.5 oz	310
Pina Colada - 4.5 oz	300
Gin/Vodka Tonic- 4.5 oz	200
Gin/Vodka Diet Tonic	100
Bloody Mary - 5 oz	116
Martini- 3 oz gin or vodka	190
Margarita - 4 oz	248

Here's the lowdown on those fancy coffee drinks. A 20-ounce Starbucks Frappucino® with whipped cream is around 430 calories—without whipped cream it is about 280 calories. Add a cheese danish or a croissant and you've got a big chunk of your daily calorie intake if you're trying to lose weight. Order fat-free, sugar-free powders, skim milk etc. to cut down on calories.

I'm not a doctor but I am a specialist in spa cuisine. I worked at Deepak Chopra's Center For Well Being, at a number of spas and have created diets for weight loss. I saw lots of people come and go. Some successfully kept the weight off and some didn't. Weight is personal and individual. We all have different body types, metabolisms and emotional conditioning which affect our mental state—that's very important when you're trying to lose weight. Gaining weight can be depressing which, in turn, prevents you from getting up the 'go' you need to start a healthy eating plan. Here's what I know. From my personal observations and experience, there are things that everyone can do to start the ball rolling.

- Forget your weight loss failures. Erase the past. Start with a clean state. Focus on here and now.
- Stop thinking that losing weight is hard. Healthy eating is not difficult especially when it becomes routine. Don't think of it as a diet. Think of it as a plan to extend your life.
- Curb hunger in-between meals with healthy snacks and it's not all carrots and celery or 'bird food.' Trust me.
- Don't beat yourself up if you do fall off the wagon. Every day is a new beginning.
- Slow down. Don't inhale your food and don't reach for that second portion. Take time to eat. It takes 20-30 minutes for body chemistry to signal when you're full.

Now I will give you my personal secret for losing weight. It's simple if you can do it. There's a lot of discipline involved. It requires courage. Many have tried but few have done it. What is it? **DON'T EAT IN YOUR CAR.** This is not conducive to health or fitness. Eating and driving is stressful, can be dangerous and is usually fattening since what you get at a drive through is loaded with calories, trans-fats, fillers, hormone injected meat, the list goes on. In the U.S., 20% of food is eaten in the car!

You can get stressed just from digesting all this information. I want to make it clear that this chapter is not intended to give you a diet plan or menus or a ton of recipes. There are lots of places on the Internet and other books that can give you those. I will remind you that before you begin any weight loss program, it's wise to consult a doctor.[6] My forte is teaching you to start cooking some great food that will help you lose weight, keep it off and stay healthy for the long term. Here are some things I cook for my clients when they're trying to slim down or just stay in shape.

A smoothie can jump start your morning or give you an afternoon energy boost. The basic ingredients are unfiltered apple juice, or whatever type of juice you like, as long as it's not loaded with sugar. Be creative with your combinations. A lot will depend on what's fresh but in a pinch, frozen is okay. This is a good way to "break the fast" after a night's sleep.

BREAKFAST SMOOTHIE

INGREDIENTS:

1 frozen ripe banana

8 oz unfiltered apple juice or orange juice

1 cup fresh or frozen fruit or a combination of strawberries, pineapple, blueberries, raspberries, peaches (or your favorite)

Serves 2

DIRECTIONS:

1. Break up the banana into pieces and put them in a blender.
2. Add the apple juice and fruit(s).
3. Mix until smooth.

OPTIONS TO ADD:

- Protein powder
- Powdered vitamin mixes
- Wheat germ
- Yogurt

---

[6]. All information in this chapter is intended for your general knowledge only and is not a substitute for medical advice or treatment for specific medical conditions.

GORDON'S TIP: *When freezing bananas, be sure to peel them first, then put them in an air-tight zip lock.*

Steaming is my preferred way to cook vegetables. Don't boil them since they lose nutrients and flavor. Here's how you can steam perfect veggies every time. Remember I said the density of the vegetable is important to timing? A carrot is thick, a zucchini is soft inside and a mushroom is spongy. Cook these in stages or layer with the densest at the bottom. You'll be surprised how much natural taste vegetables have. If you don't like the ones in this recipe, change them. It's your food reality.

STEAMED VEGGIE MANIA

INGREDIENTS:

1 cup fresh broccoli florets

1 cup cauliflower florets

2 medium carrots, sliced

2 medium zucchini, sliced

1 cup mushrooms, washed & sliced

Salt and pepper to taste

Prep time: 15 minutes

Serves 4

DIRECTIONS:

1. Place steamer into a large pot. Water should be just below the basket bottom. Bring water to a rapid boil.
2. Layer the vegetables with the carrots at the bottom, broccoli and zucchini next and mushrooms on top.
3. Steam for 10 minutes or until tender.
4. Remove steamer and turn onto a serving dish.

- *Steam a piece of salmon or some shrimp on top of the vegetables*
- *Season with reduced sodium soy sauce, lemon juice, extra virgin olive oil*
- *Use as a side dish with leftover chicken or turkey*

GORDON SAYS: *If you want to make extra to save in plastic bags, rinse, then plunge them into very cold water so they stop cooking. When you're ready to eat them, steam them for a few minutes. DON'T MICROWAVE VEGETABLES—it overcooks them.*

Remember, salmon is a rich source of Omega-3s which may be helpful in prevention of heart problems. While it's on the oily side, this recipe doesn't add any fat and the calories are great.

TIPS FOR BAKING SALMON

You can bake salmon but be aware of the cut.
- Filets take less time than salmon steaks.
- Fish cooks fast and is best baked at a high temperature to kill bacteria…no lower than 375°.
- For each inch of thickness, figure 10 minutes or 15 – 25 minutes if wrapped in foil or parchment paper.
- Don't salt salmon before cooking because it makes it too dry.
- Test for doneness by pressing the flesh with a fork. It's done when it doesn't feel soft and is more resistant.
- Cooked salmon is pink with white lines.

GORDON SAYS: *Using cooking spray cuts down the oil. I like coconut oil. The less fat you have, the better. Also, if you don't like dill, you can use grated ginger or serve it plain with lemon.*

This is a good dish for a busy guy. It takes 20 minutes to prepare and cook.

SENSATIONAL SALMON BROIL

INGREDIENTS:

4 salmon fillets (4 oz each)

1/2 cup fat-free mayo

2 tablespoons fresh lime juice

2 tablespoons fresh lemon juice

1 tablespoon Dijon mustard

1 tablespoon chopped dill

Serves 4

MARINADE:

Make a marinade by combining the lemon and lime juices. Put the salmon in the bowl for 10 minutes. Turn once to coat fully.

DIRECTIONS

1. Pre-heat broiler.
2. Mix the mustard, mayo and dill in a small bowl. Set aside.
3. Coat the broiler pan with cooking spray. Remove the salmon from the marinade and pat dry.
4. Broil the salmon on the rack about 4" from the heat.
5. Cook about 4 minutes or until salmon flakes in the center. Don't overcook or it will be too dry.
6. Serve on a plate and cover each fillet with the mustard-dill sauce.

Roast chicken is nutritious, great protein for weight loss and gives you plenty of leftovers. Novice cooks can overcook and dry out chicken. Ovens have different calibrations; yours could be off. An oven thermometer can give you an accurate reading but the best way to tell if poultry is done is by the internal temperature: 180°. Add a food thermometer to your kitchen utensil drawer. I'm probably going to get a lot of heat from chefs for this next tip but one foolproof way I know to make succulent roast chicken is to cook it in one of those Reynolds bags you get in the supermarket. The steam helps retain the juices and you can make a delicious natural gravy (au jus) that collects in the bottom of the bag. Yes, the skin does get crisp. Cleanup is easy. No messy pans; just throw the bag away!

IT'S IN THE BAG...CHICKEN & VEGETABLES

INGREDIENTS:

1 Reynolds® Large Oven Bag (16"x17-1/2")

1 tablespoon flour

4 to 5 lb whole chicken

1 teaspoon garlic salt, divided

1 lb baby red potatoes, unpeeled

1 package (8 oz) peeled baby carrots

2 stalks celery, cut in 1/2-inch slices

1 medium onion, cut into quarters

1 tablespoon oil

1 teaspoon paprika

A tasty option is to put a cut lemon in the cavity of the chicken.

Serves 4

DIRECTIONS:

1. Preheat oven to 350°.
2. Shake flour and 1/2 teaspoon garlic salt in the bag. Place in a 13"x 9"x 2" baking pan.
3. Place vegetables in the oven bag. Turn bag to mix vegetables with seasoned flour; push vegetables to the outer edge of the bag.
4. Brush chicken with oil, if desired. Sprinkle and rub chicken with remaining garlic salt and paprika.
5. Place chicken in the center of vegetables in the bag.
6. Close oven bag with nylon tie; cut six 1/2-inch slits in top.
7. Bake until chicken is tender, 1-1/4 to 1-1/2 hours until meat thermometer inserted in chicken reads 180°F.

A lot of recipes online give the first step as "rinse chicken and pat dry." Don't do it!! The USDA Food Safety Division recently warned that washing raw poultry or any meat before cooking it is NOT recommended. Some bacteria can be easily washed off and poultry juices splashed on the surfaces of your kitchen can be spread to other foods, utensils and surfaces causing cross-contamination. Cooking (baking, broiling, boiling, and grilling) to the right temperature kills the bacteria, so washing chicken is not necessary.[7]

---

7. www.fsis.usda.gov/factsheets/Does_Washing_Food_Promote_Food_Safety/

This next recipe uses Marsala wine which is an Italian sherry. Cooking with alcohol enhances flavor and the acid helps tenderize meat and poultry. Alcohol has a lower boiling point than water but it doesn't all burn off. The amount of alcohol and the cooking time are what will determine how much remains; simmering for 30 minutes leaves about 35%. A wine-based stew cooking for 2 hours retains 10%.[8] Those foods flambéed with flair at your table retain 75% of their alcohol. This chart indicates how much alcohol is burned off in cooking.

ALCOHOL BURN OFF CHART

Preparation Method	Percent Retained
Alcohol added to boiling liquid & removed from heat	85%
Alcohol flamed	75%
No heat, stored overnight	70%
Baked, 25 minutes, alcohol not stirred into mixture	45%
Baked/simmered dishes with alcohol stirred into mixture:	
15 minutes cooking time	40%
30 minutes cooking time	35%
1 hour cooking time	25%
1.5 hours cooking time	20%
2 hours cooking time	10%
2.5 hours cooking time	5%

If you can't have alcohol, you can substitute orange or pineapple juice or extracts for the Marsala wine. Chicken or beef stock can also be substituted for white and red wines in other recipes.

---

8. U.S. Department of Agriculture Alcohol burn-off chart

CHICKEN MARSALA

INGREDIENTS:

4 boneless chicken breasts

1 teaspoon butter

3 tablespoons chicken broth

4 large mushrooms, sliced

3 tablespoons Marsala or sherry wine

2 tablespoons water

Serves 4

PREPARATION:

Put the chicken breast between 2 wax paper pieces and pound it thin. This is called a paillard. If you don't have a wooden mallet, use any flat ended heavy object, like a 5 pound dumbbell.

DIRECTIONS

1. Melt the butter and add the mushrooms. Sprinkle with salt and pepper. When the mushrooms are soft, remove them to a bowl and set aside.

2. Add the pounded chicken breasts and cook over medium heat until they are browned on both sides. Remove the chicken and set aside.

3. Stir the wine, water and stock into the juices in the skillet.

4. Return the chicken to the skillet. Reduce the heat and simmer for 5 minutes.

5. Add the mushrooms. Simmer 1 minute more.

6. Serve hot with steamed veggies.

GORDON SAYS: *To change the flavor, change the herbs. Substitute basil with tarragon or rosemary. Greeks love oregano. Add some grated fresh ginger. Educate your palate. See what you like. If you don't like broccoli, use something else. Be the master of your food domain.*

Soup is my favorite way to shed weight that has crept up on me. One of the best ways to cut back without feeling hungry is to eat a hearty soup in place of a meal. With this next recipe, you're not only cutting calories but you're getting a lot of vital nutrients to keep up your strength.

POUNDS OFF SOUP

INGREDIENTS:

- 3 cans of light chicken broth
- 1 tablespoon vegetable oil
- 1/4 cup raw barley
- 2 cloves garlic, chopped
- 1 large onion, chopped
- 2 carrots, sliced
- 1 celery stalk, chopped
- 1 potato, cut into bite-sized chunks
- 1 cup broccoli florets
- 1/2 teaspoon black pepper
- 1/4 cup minced fresh basil

Optional: Add Jalapeño pepper, seeded and chopped and/ or chicken breast strips.

DIRECTIONS:

1. In a large stock pot, heat oil over medium heat. Stir in onions, garlic and barley.
2. Cook until onions are soft.
3. Add the chicken broth, vegetables, pepper, and basil.
4. Simmer 1 hour over medium low/heat.
5. Serve hot.

Serves 4

"An army marches on its stomach. Soup makes the soldier."

—Napoleon Bonaparte, French Emperor, General

Macaroni and cheese are a single man's staple. The kind you buy in the box is full of chemicals and additives. The kind your mother made is high fat and loaded with calories. Here's a good recipe that's healthier, has fewer calories but still tastes good.

GOOD FOR YOU MACARONI AND CHEESE

INGREDIENTS:

2 tablespoons olive oil

2 tablespoons Wondra flour

1/2 cup non-fat milk

1 pound elbow macaroni

1 cup reduced fat grated or shredded Cheddar cheese*

*My favorite is smoked Gouda.

Serves 4

DIRECTIONS:

COOK THE PASTA:

Bring a large pot of salted water to a rolling boil. Add macaroni to the water and cook about 7 or 8 minutes.

Drain the pasta. Rinse immediately with cold water and coat with a few drops of olive oil to keep it from sticking together.

1. Preheat oven to 375°.
2. Spray a 2 quart casserole with nonstick cooking spray.
3. Heat the milk. DON'T BOIL IT. Set aside.
4. Put the oil in a saucepan. Add the Wondra.
5. Mix with a whisk over medium heat, slowly adding the hot milk.
6. Simmer for 5 minutes. Stir a few times.
7. Stir the grated cheese into the milk.
8. Salt and pepper to taste. Set aside.
9. Put the macaroni into the casserole dish and stir in the milk mixture.
10. Sprinkle the top with more grated cheese.
11. Bake, uncovered, for about 3 minutes or until edges are bubbling.
12. Remove from the oven and let stand about 10 minutes before serving.

I have one more word for you. Tofu. I can hear those groans through the pages. Tofu is what your vegetarian friend orders that you'd never share. Why am I mentioning this? Tofu is good for weight loss. It's low in saturated fat, high is protein, low carb and has nutritional value too: vitamin B, calcium, iron and all 8 essential amino acids. So what is it? Tofu is made by coagulating soy milk, then pressing the curds into spongy white blocks: firm, extra firm and silken, used to make things creamy, like dips. Tofu is almost tasteless but absorbs the flavors and spices of any recipe. When cooking, press out the water with a towel before you slice, dice, chop or crumble it. It can be baked, broiled, fried, added to soups and casseroles, and is even used to make desserts. Try it. You might like it!

TANTALIZING TOFU LASAGNA

INGREDIENTS:

8 oz box lasagna noodles*

6 oz package firm tofu, drained & rinsed

1 cup shredded low-fat mozzarella cheese

1 cup grated parmesan cheese

1 cup ricotta cheese

1/8 cup milk

2 eggs, lightly beaten

2 cups spaghetti sauce

1/2 teaspoon dried parsley

1/2 teaspoon salt

Pepper to taste

You can look for the no-boil kind that are all ready to go.

DIRECTIONS:

1. Cook and drain the lasagna noodles. Add a tablespoon of oil to keep from sticking.
2. Preheat oven to 350°.
3. Crumble the tofu and mix with the mozzarella, ricotta, parsley, milk, salt and pepper.
4. Spread a layer of sauce in the bottom of a 9x13 inch baking dish. Arrange noodles lengthwise over the sauce. Top with more sauce.
5. Spread a layer of the ricotta cheese mixture over the noodles and top with a layer of sauce. Sprinkle with parmesan cheese.
6. Repeat the layers and top end the last one with mozzarella and parmesan cheese.
7. Cover with foil. To prevent sticking to the cheese, spray the inside with cooking spray.
8. Bake 25 minutes.
9. Remove foil, let stand 5 minutes and serve.

Serves 6

Tofu is a good meat substitute and there are two others I like to use. Seitan is popular with vegetarians but it's made from wheat so it's not gluten-free. It's good for you because a four-ounce serving has 26 grams of protein, only 2 grams of fat and no cholesterol. One big plus is that it looks and cooks like meat. Seitan is the main ingredient in Tofurkey but on Thanksgiving you don't get a wishbone!

Tempeh is made from fermented, cooked soybeans. One of my most popular dishes everyone loves on a buffet table is tempeh with peanut sauce. Don't be intimidated by the amount of ingredients. With the exception of cumin and coriander, you probably have most of them in your kitchen already.

TEMPTING TEMPEH WITH PEANUT SAUCE

INGREDIENTS:

8 oz package tempeh, cut into 1/2" slices

2 tablespoons peanut oil or vegetable oil

2 tablespoons tamari or soy sauce

1/3 cup creamy peanut butter*

3 scallions, chopped

2 teaspoons ginger, minced

1 teaspoon garlic, minced

14 oz can unsweetened coconut milk

1 tablespoon lime juice

1 teaspoon light brown sugar

1/4 teaspoon cayenne, or to taste

1/4 teaspoon cumin

1/4 teaspoon coriander powder

1/4 cup peanuts, chopped

2 tablespoons cilantro, minced

*Get organic if available

DIRECTIONS:

1. Poach the tempeh in a skillet of simmering water for 15 minutes.
2. Drain and blot dry.
3. Heat the oil in the same skillet over medium high heat.
4. Add tempeh and 1 tablespoon of the tamari for color and flavor.
5. Cook until browned on all sides. Set aside.
6. In a food processor or blender, combine the peanut butter, scallions, ginger, garlic, coconut milk, lime juice, brown sugar, cayenne, cumin and coriander and remaining tablespoon of tamari. Process until smooth.
7. Stir the sauce into the skillet with the tempeh and simmer until hot and slightly reduced, about 7 to 10 minutes.
8. Serve over brown rice. Garnish with chopped peanuts and cilantro.

Serves 6

To wrap up this chapter, let's review a few weight loss myths:

- Fad diets work for permanent weight loss ☞ **FALSE**
- Going vegetarian guarantees that you will lose weight ☞ **FALSE**
- Certain foods burn fat, like grapefruit or celery ☞ **FALSE**
- Cutting out fat cuts calories ☞ **FALSE**
- Skipping meals helps you lose weight ☞ **FALSE**
- Cut out all starches if you want to lose weight ☞ **FALSE**
- To lose weight, burn more calories than you consume ☞ **TRUE**

You don't have to become a monk or cut out food that has taste to eat well and weigh less. After you get to a healthy weight, you'll look and feel better. You'll be revved up and ready to go. In the next chapter, we'll party healthy... really. Remember that alcohol has hidden calories. If you fall off the wagon, I have a natural hangover cure to get you back in the driver's seat again!

CHAPTER

PARTY HEALTHY

Everyone loves a party. It's a great way to be with friends and let off steam. There are so many occasions—so much food. What's usually on those festive tables are dishes loaded with fat and calories, i.e., nutritional Armageddon. What can you do if you are trying to keep that cholesterol down, lose weight or just want to avoid that oh-so-familiar heartburn after too many weird combinations? Party food tastes good but can clog your arteries or make you run for the Rolaids. Besides the unhealthy fare, we tend to overeat at a party because it's a fun event. Sometimes we're attached to foods because they evoke certain sense memories. That's right. Your brain remembers food that connects to certain life experiences like hamburgers sizzling on the grill, broiling that big catch over a campfire, ice cold beer on a broiling hot day. "Food triggers" can also cause you to overeat. The most common ones are sugary and calorie dense like ice cream, French fries, potato chips with that famous challenge: "Bet you can't eat just one." Smell and environments are other factors—walking into a movie theater with the tantalizing aroma of popcorn, ordering that extra butter, hot dogs at the ball game, the favorite meal your Mom cooks when you visit. Good times and bad ones can also set off a binge. These are emotional triggers.

What does this have to do with Party Healthy? Everything. You can have a blast and throw a healthy party without your buddies laughing their asses off. I know…you hate the word healthy. How about you are what you eat, as the saying goes. Do you really see yourself as a package of plaque or a load of lard? So let me show you ways you can have some really great appetizers and party food without your macho friends thinking it's a junk food intervention.

Later, we'll give you some guidelines about what to do when you are invited to a party with all those yummy, greasy nostalgia foods and tips for take out…we'll get to those later.

GORDON SAYS: *On Super Bowl Sunday, Americans eat about 8 million pounds of guacamole. Avocados have gotten a bad rap but don't fear the fat…it's a good one.*

Avocados are the only fruit that has mono-unsaturated fat which actually speeds up your metabolism. They're packed with vitamins, minerals, anti-oxidants and are a good source of potassium and folate, nutrients important to circulation and heart health. They also have phytonutrients, chemical compounds that could help prevent heart diseases and other chronic illnesses[1]. There are more than 80 varieties of avocados. The most common is the year-round Hass avocado, whose original mother tree still stands in California, the largest avocado producing state.

---

1. USDA.GOV Archive 12/99 "Phytonutrients Take Center Stage"

Here's a great recipe for a party or to use as a great condiment on tacos or other Mexican dishes.

GOOD FOR YOU GUACAMOLE

INGREDIENTS:

2 medium ripe avocados

4 tablespoons uncooked red onion, chopped

4 tablespoons cilantro, fresh, chopped

2 tablespoons fresh lime juice

1/2 teaspoon table salt, or to taste

1/4 teaspoon hot pepper sauce or to taste.

2 tomatoes, chopped or 1/2 cup salsa

Serves 4 (double it for large groups)

DIRECTIONS:

1. Scoop out the avocado meat and mash with a fork until almost smooth.
2. Add the remaining ingredients and stir until combined.
3. Sprinkle with lemon juice to keep from turning brown. Cover with plastic wrap and refrigerate up to 1 day.
4. Serve with baked chips or on cucumber slices.

GORDON'S TIP: *Squeezing an avocado can bruise it. To see if it's ripe, flick the small brown stem off the top. If it comes off easily and you can see green underneath, it's ready!*

The Super Bowl and other end-of-season games are a great get together. It's not just about who wins or loses…it's also about the food. Chili is a great staple. Here's a recipe that your buddies will enjoy. They won't even know it's turkey! You can make this in advance and reheat it in a crock pot or on low heat. Watch the clock. Stir to avoid burning.

TERRIFIC TURKEY CHILI

INGREDIENTS:

1-1/2 teaspoons olive oil

1 lb ground turkey

1 onion, chopped

2 cups water

1 can canned crushed tomatoes (28 oz)

1 can canned kidney beans, drained, rinsed and mashed (16 oz)

1 tablespoon garlic, minced

2 tablespoons chili powder

1/2 teaspoon paprika

1/2 teaspoon dried oregano

1/2 teaspoon ground cayenne pepper

1/2 teaspoon salt

1/2 teaspoon ground black pepper

Serves 8

DIRECTIONS:

1. Heat the oil in a large pot over medium heat.
2. Place ground turkey in the pot, crumbling with a fork until evenly browned.
3. Stir in onion and cook 5 more minutes.
4. Pour water into the pot.
5. Mix in tomatoes, kidney beans, and garlic.
6. Add seasonings: chili powder, paprika, oregano, cayenne, salt, and pepper.
7. Bring to a boil. Reduce to low heat, cover, and simmer for 30 minutes.

One thing you need to know when giving a party is how to change the number of servings. This is called scaling a recipe. Great websites for this are www.allrecipes.com or www.delish.com. Each recipe has a serving size, but click "Change Serving Size" and you can immediately adjust the recipe! It's a great feature! Check out this free online convertor

www.free-online-calculator-use.com/recipe-conversion-calculator.html#calculator

An added benefit of that chili recipe is in the beans. They are truly a powerhouse food. Just one cup of beans can have as much as 16 grams of protein. They're also a great source of fiber, potassium and calcium. Some studies show that eating beans on a regular basis can reduce the risk of diabetes, heart disease, cancer and obesity. In one study reported in the Archives of Internal Medicine, men and women who consumed legumes four times a week had a 22% lower risk for heart disease than did people consuming legumes only once.[2]

What about that old saying, "Beans, beans, the musical fruit, the more you eat the more you toot." The true "fart fact" is that beans contain sugars the human body has a hard time digesting. Canning removes some of the gas-causing sugars and coating but you should still rinse beans before eating them. If you are preparing dried beans, soak them and rinse before cooking. Guys, don't overdo your portions; increase your bean consumption gradually. Right now, let's make some of my party favorites that won't brand you a health nut!

SENSATIONAL SEVEN LAYER BEAN DIP

INGREDIENTS:

- 2 cans fat-free refried beans (16 oz each)
- 1 cup salsa
- 2 cups fat-free shredded Cheddar cheese
- 2 cups fat-free sour cream
- 4 medium tomatoes, chopped
- 2 tablespoons fresh cilantro, finely chopped
- 1/2 cup red onion, chopped
- 4 tablespoons pitted black olives, chopped

Serves 32 (half recipe for less)

DIRECTIONS:

1. Mix together the refried beans and salsa.
2. Spread this bean mixture on the bottom of a 9"x13" baking dish.
3. Spread a layer of sour cream on the bean layer, then layer the shredded cheese.
4. Last, layer tomatoes, onions, cilantro and olives on top.
5. You can cover and refrigerate for up to 4 hours.
6. Serve with baked tortilla chips.

---

2. www.usdrybeans.com/nutrition/benefits

WONDROUS WHITE BEAN DIP

INGREDIENTS:

2 15oz cans cannellini beans (white kidney beans), rinsed

1/2 cup extra-virgin olive oil

1 tablespoon lemon juice

1/2 teaspoon salt

1/2 cup scallions, chopped

1 tablespoon fresh dill, chopped

Black & cayenne pepper to taste

Serves 10

DIRECTIONS:

1. Rinse and drain the cannellini beans.
2. Combine beans, olive oil, lemon juice, cayenne, salt and black pepper in a blender or food processor.
3. Process until smooth.
4. Scrape into a bowl; stir in scallions and dill.
5. Serve with cut veggies or baked chips.

GORDON SAYS: *Nuts are a smart, nutritious addition to a party instead of a bowl of candy. Get raw or unsalted ones and you can roast them with your own seasonings.*

QUICK BLACK BEAN DIP

INGREDIENTS:

1 can refried beans (16 oz)

1 package taco seasoning (1.25 oz)

1 tomato, chopped

1 cup and 1 tablespoon Cheddar cheese, shredded low-fat

Serves 10

DIRECTIONS:

1. In a medium saucepan mix refried beans, taco seasoning mix and tomato.
2. Simmer over medium heat, approximately 20 minutes, stirring occasionally.
3. Spoon into a bowl and top with cheese.
4. Serve with baked chips.

A great low-fat dip is hummus, available in most supermarkets. It's made from garbanzo beans and comes in a wide variety of flavors like roasted red pepper, basil pesto, sun-dried tomato or roasted garlic. Try it with baked pita chips or vegetables.

I really love chicken wings but they are high in calories and fat because they're battered and fried. Here's how I make them party healthy. My friends can't get enough of them.

GORDON'S WINGS

INGREDIENTS:

3 lbs chicken wings (do not rinse)

2 cups sweet chili sauce, available in Asian section.*

*If you can't find store-bought sauce, you can make your own from online recipes.

Serves 12

DIRECTIONS:

1. Marinate wings in sauce for several hours.
2. Preheat oven to 375°.
3. Grease a baking dish with cooking spray.
4. Place chicken in baking dish.
5. Bake for one hour.
6. Serve warm.

You can make this in advance and reheat.

GORDON'S TIP: *Cut off the wing tip and cut where the bone is joined to the wing. This will give you two pieces.*

You can also bake the wings in ready-made Teriyaki sauce but here's an easy marinade you can make yourself.

TERIYAKI MARINADE

Mix together:
- 1 cup soy sauce
- 1/2 cup brown sugar
- 2 garlic cloves, minced
- 1 teaspoon ground ginger

Nachos are a party staple but you don't have to break the cheesy cholesterol bank if you follow my recipe. This satisfies your nacho cravings but makes it heart friendly by cutting down the fat and calories.

MACHO NACHOS

INGREDIENTS:

Reduced-fat or multigrain tortilla chips

2 teaspoons olive oil

2 cups pinto beans, drained and rinsed*

1 tablespoon cilantro, chopped

3 tablespoons lime juice

8 oz reduced-fat, shredded Cheddar cheese

Toppings: Sliced avocado, chopped tomatoes, Salsa (green or red), chopped olives

*Can also use black beans or white cannellini

Serves 8

DIRECTIONS:

1. In a medium bowl, mash beans with olive oil, lime juice and cilantro.
2. Place corn chips in a large ovenproof plate or baking dish.
3. Spoon bean mixture over chips, then sprinkle with cheese.
4. Bake, uncovered, about 10 minutes or until cheese is melted.
5. Top with salsa, chopped olives or serve toppings on the side.

I make my own tortilla chips and it's easier than you think. You can use flour or corn but here's the 'skinny' on the difference for an 8-9" round:

- Flour Tortilla................... 120 calories .... 3.5 grams of fat
- Low Carb Tortilla .... 70 calories .... 2.5 grams of fat
- Corn Tortilla .... 30 calories .... 1.5 grams of fat

Remember low carb doesn't mean low calorie!

MY TORTILLA CHIPS

INGREDIENTS:

8 corn tortillas

Nonstick oil spray

Salt to taste

Note: Watch carefully as they can burn easily. Chips will continue to crisp when they cool.

Serves ?

DIRECTIONS:

1. Preheat oven to 400°.
2. Lightly spray the tortillas on both sides.
3. Stack the tortillas and cut into quarters.
4. Spread the triangles in a single layer on a cookie sheet.
5. Bake 5-6 minutes until edges start to curl.

My personal chip choice is from family owned Beanfields Snacks. Reed and Liza Glidden created a great alternative to any regular chip because they're made from beans and rice with bonus points for nutrition. A one-ounce serving has 4 grams of protein and 4 grams of fiber—twice as much as most other tortilla chips, corn chips or potato chips. They're corn-free and non-GMO! They come in five flavors but my favorite is nacho. Use these instead of tortilla chips to punch up the flavor of any recipe. Ask for it in your local health food store or you order them online at www.beanfieldssnacks.com. Don't forget my Good for You Macaroni and Cheese recipe in Chapter 4. That fills up the beefiest guys and kids give it high marks!

Man cannot live on chip and dip alone. Here is a hearty appetizer slider that substitutes turkey slices for ground beef.

GAME DAY DELI SLIDERS

INGREDIENTS:

24 dinner rolls or sweet Hawaiian rolls

1 cup onion, chopped

1/2 cup butter

2 tablespoons Dijon mustard

1 tablespoon Worcestershire sauce

1 pound thinly sliced turkey

Reduced-fat Swiss cheese or provolone (cut to fit)

Variation: 1/2 cup pesto (You can get it at most stores. Spread the bottom layer with the pesto for added flavor. My recipe is in Chapter 2.)

Serves 12

DIRECTIONS:

1. Preheat oven to 350°.
2. Sauté onion in butter over low heat for 5 minutes.
3. Line a 9" x 13" baking pan with just the bottom halves of the rolls.
4. Fold a slice of turkey on each half.
5. Next add a layer of onions and then add the cheese.
6. Cover with foil and bake 20 minutes.

PARTY HEARTY!

Giving a party gives you control over what you serve, but what about when you get invited to a party? Your host may not care about saving you and there are always lots of tempting foods that are hard to resist. Here are a few tips to keep you from gorging on not-so-good-for-you party fare.

- Eat something light before you leave home, like a cup of soup, a handful of nuts, a piece of fruit, or drink a glass of water so you aren't starving when you get there.
- Scope out the food. There may actually be a few better-for-you items.

On most buffet tables, there is usually a salad and a crudité platter (fancy name for raw veggies). Put those on your plate first.

- Don't hover around the table. Take just one trip.
- If you want to eat some junk food, okay…just don't overdo it. Take a few bites to satisfy your craving. A little does go a long way.
- Beware the chicken wings! One fried, battered piece is about 200 calories. How many would fill you up?
- Cheese and crackers add up. I always eat more cheese and crackers than I should because I can't judge the portion sizes. Eat a few pieces and walk away. Not what you would normally do, but do it.
- Don't pig out on desserts. You only need a small portion; it's usually the first few bites that are the best. Pick a fruit tart over a piece of seven layer cake.

GORDON SAYS: *These are some of my favorite recipes but you can find more on the internet by putting "healthy" in front of what you want to make!*

Let's recap a few basics to remember:

✔ Serve lean meats or fish. They are lower in fat and high in protein like cooked shrimp served with cocktail sauce, roasted sliced turkey breast and sliced lean roast beef. Serve with whole grain breads.

✔ Use low-fat or fat-free yogurt in dip recipes instead of sour cream or mayonnaise.

✔ Use low-fat cheese in recipes instead of full-fat varieties.

- ✔ If you are a Helmann's "real" mayo die-hard, get the "light" or low-fat variety.
- ✔ A good substitute for mayonnaise without sacrificing taste is Vegenaise®, available in most health food stores. It's vegan, gluten-free, fat-free, dairy-free, non-GMO but does have soy. That should answer any questions about it!
- ✔ Stay away from Miracle Whip® which adds high-fructose corn syrup and sugar to the basic mayo recipe.

I have created my own recipe which is low calorie and vegan. I'll share the secret with you here. It never fails to get raves even from the most die-hard onion dip fans or meat and potatoes guys.

CHEF GORDON'S SAUCE

2 cups Vegenaise

1/4 cup nutritional yeast

4 tablespoons fresh squeezed lemon juice

Combine in a bowl and refrigerate. Serve with veggies. Keeps up to 2 weeks in the refrigerator.

TAKE OUT TIPS FOR PARTY FOOD:

So, if you have to bring something to a party, there's some decent prepared food you can pick up at a supermarket deli or a Trader Joe's (if you're lucky enough to have one in your area). And I even have a recommendation if you have a hankering for KFC®, Taco Bell®, Subway® or Dominos®. Here are some things you can do to feel better about your fast food cravings.

- ✔ Pick grilled chicken over fried. One KFC extra crispy chicken breast is 490 calories; grilled is 220.
- ✔ Choose a garden salad over the Caesar which is a higher fat dressing. Ask for reduced-fat dressing.
- ✔ Get soft tacos instead of the crispy shell and black beans instead of refried.
- ✔ Cut your foot long sandwich down to 6" on whole grain bread with lean

meat. Hold the mayo and use mustard. Ask for a low-fat cheese like Swiss or Mozzarella and pile on the veggies.

✔ Order your pizza packed with veggie toppers. Hard core meat lovers, get pepperoni, or ask for chicken sausage or BBQ chicken.

THE BOOZE YOU CHOOSE!

In chapter four we talked about alcohol as it relates to weight loss, something you should also be aware of on the party scene. We're drinking to have fun and we can easily lose track of how many drinks we down during the night. Here's how it can make you gain. When we drink on an empty stomach the body chooses alcohol as its primary fuel. While less than 5% of the alcohol you drink is turned into fat, the main effect of alcohol is to reduce the amount of fat your body burns for energy. Coupled with the high caloric value of alcohol, the resulting effect is that body is forced to store an excessive amount of unburned fat calories.[3]

Alcohol is calorie dense but those extra belly rolls are likely to come from any calorie-dense source. Let's look at the so-called beer belly, a long-debunked, but slow to die myth.[4] As my friend Greg Koch of Stone Brewing says, "It's not the beer that adds pounds but the poor food decisions we sometimes make when we're drinking beer."

He should know. He's been a dedicated craft beer drinker for 25 plus years, yet is lean and looks considerably younger than his age. "Think about

---

3. www.rochester.edu/uhs/healthtopics/Alcohol/caloricvalues.html
4. newsfeed.time.com/2013/06/13/beer-bellies-are-a-myth/

it," Greg says. "Who profits most from the myth of the 'beer belly'? The industrial brewers, that's who. They want to use less ingredients in their beer, charge you the same amount and have you thank them for it. I'd bet anything that if a comprehensive study was conducted between industrial light beer drinkers and craft beer drinkers you'd find that on average light beer drinkers are heavier. It's like the person sucking down diet soda while eating fast food. If you disconnect the reality of total caloric input and instead let the television commercials make your decisions for you, it won't help you get where you want to go. Put another way, it's my belief that if you drink so much beer that calories are the problem, then it's not calories that are your problem… it's possibly alcoholism. In which case, seek help."

Responsible moderate enjoyment of good quality craft beer is, in my opinion, part of a quality lifestyle. Eat real food. Enjoy real beer. Leave the industrialized notions of food I'm totally onboard with Greg. There's also serving size to consider. Both cans and bottles of beer average 12-ounces, while a glass of wine is 5-ounces and a shot glass is just 1.5-ounces. Follow the logic here. If the average drinker consumed wine in greater quantities than beer, the myth might have focused on a 'wine belly.' Cut down the number of beers you drink. Five or six can have as many calories as a whole meal. Calories are not targeted missiles that know how to go to one area so why is the belly always mentioned? One reason could be the development of ascites, a buildup of fluid from excessive alcohol consumption that can cause your abdomen to swell and can indicate liver damage. [5] Most likely a 'belly' comes from overeating and lack of exercise! All that said, if you want to know the calories in some of those commercial yellow fizzy beers, here's a chart. Don't get fooled by thinking anything labeled 'light' is healthier… it's not![6]

> **"Men hate the taste of beer to begin with. It is, however, a prejudice that many people have been able to overcome."**
>
> —Winston Churchill, British former Prime Minister

---

5. www.medicinenet.com/ascites/article.htm
6. www.fitsugar.com/Calories-Popular-Beers-1504697

Brand	Calories	Carbs (g)	% Alcohol
Amstel Light	95	5	3.5
Budweiser	145	10.6	5
Bud Light	110	6.6	4.2
Coors	149	12.2	5
Coors Light	102	5	4.2
Corona	148	14	4.6
Corona Light	99	5	3.2
Guinness Stout	176	14	6
Guinness Draught	126	10	4
Heineken	148	11.3	5
Heineken Light	99	6.8	3.5
Miller Genuine Draft	143	13.1	4.7
Miller MGD 64	64	2.4	2.8
Sam Adams	180	18.8	4.9
Sam Adams Light	119	9.6	4
Stella Artois	154	11.6	5.2

Craft beer is all the rage now because the brewers actually focus on quality rather than just the watering down industrialization of most mass-produced brands. Artisan beer principally focuses on barley, wheat, hops and water. This is like eating whole-grain instead of cheap white bread. A good craft beer also has some nutritional value, about 2.2 grams protein, 195 mg potassium, and 5% to 15% of the daily intake for riboflavin, niacin, folic acid and vitamin B-6. Don't try to substitute a cold one for a good breakfast or think you can live on beer alone just because historically, monks fasted with beer! Some craft beer can have an alcohol content higher than the diluted brands (4%-11%) but there's a plus…you can get a good buzz after one or two instead of the four or five of the watered-down brewskis which make you drain the lizard more often. Remember that when you're just about to make your move and you have to run to the men's room!

My hands-down favorite craft beer is from Stone Brewing Co. located in Escondido, in San Diego County. Co-Founders Greg Koch and Steve Wagner and

their team are true artisan brew masters. The logos alone are party worthy: Stone Ruination IPA, Arrogant Bastard Ale, Stone Levitation Ale and Stone Sublimely Self-Righteous Ale. Stone is the largest brewery in Southern California. If you're in the area, they have a cool tour of the brewery and two eclectic, expansive farm-to-table restaurants. As of 2012, Stone was the 10th largest craft brewery and 17th largest overall brewery in the United States.[7] Check out these websites for Stone in your area. www.stonebrewing.com www.stoneworldbistro.com

Cocktails were covered in the weight loss chapter but here's a refresher and some additional things to remember. Mixed drinks are a red flag because they mask how much you're consuming and the alcohol could be a brand you'd never drink straight. At a party most mixers are low quality and often loaded with sugar. It's best to eat before drinking because liquor consumed on an empty stomach is absorbed straight into the bloodstream and the liver can't handle it…it's a fast drunk. Beer is the worst offender; carbonation speeds up absorption.

SERVING SIZE	CALORIES
Scotch 1 oz	65
Mai Tai 4.5 oz	310
Pina Colada 4.5 oz	300
Gin/Vodka Tonic 4.5 ox	200
Gin/Vodka Diet Tonic	100
Bloody Mary 5 oz	116
Martini 3 oz gin or vodka	190
Margarita 4 oz	248
Sake 4 oz	157

---

7. www.brewersassociation.org/

"Drunkenness is simply voluntary insanity."
—Seneca, Roman philosopher and statesman

Ever wonder why you get a hangover? Alcohol rapidly drops your blood sugar and you urinate more…that causes dehydration. Your body chemistry is also reacting to the toxic chemical in alcohol (acetaldehyde). You start feeling the symptoms: dizziness, nausea, light sensitivity, headaches, muscle aches.

Here are some myths about what can cure a hangover:

- "Hair of the Dog," i.e., more alcohol: This is a bad idea. A Bloody Mary sounds good but it's not a vegetable juice cure.

- Coffee: Caffeine narrows blood vessels and boosts blood pressure aggravating the hangover. If you are a regular coffee drinker, take a small cup and wait a half hour to see if you feel better.

- Pain medications: Ibuprofen could help aches and pains. Avoid Tylenol® (acetaminophen). It metabolizes in the liver and yours is already working overtime from the booze. Aspirin thins the blood. Ask your doctor what pain medication is right for you.

- Exercise: Nope. Sweating it out will dehydrate you even more.

- Sports drinks. You do lose some electrolytes but not enough to matter unless you are a very heavy drinker.

- Greasy foods: What do you think?

- Energy Boosters: Don't even think about it. They will dehydrate you even more and make you anxious. Not good for sleep either. A 5 hour energy shot has 200 mg of caffeine, Red Bull® has 80 mg, Monster® has 16 mg and Cocaine® energy drink (the actual name) has 280 mg. A cup of coffee only has 49 mg of caffeine.

- Sex: Sorry to report that no research confirms it's a hangover cure but you will feel pretty good anyway afterwards!

So what does work?

- ☞ Water: The elixir of life can restore yours. Drink water before you go to bed and grab a bottle in the morning too. Remember, you are dehydrated so no need to worry about a bathroom call when sleeping.

- ☞ Fruit Juices: They contain vitamins and natural sugar (fructose) that can help wake up your groggy metabolism.

- ☞ Eggs: They are chock full of amino acids including taurine which boosts liver function.

- ☞ Sleep: Hangovers are worse if you don't get enough sleep. Alcohol interrupts your cycle so while you may fall asleep fast, most likely you'll wake up in the middle of the night. When you do, drink water and go back to sleep.

Chicago scientists and doctors collaborated on a hangover cure and opened a clinic called "Revive." Subjects were tested and a personal 'cocktail' was placed in an IV bag which contained vitamins, potassium, calcium and an anti-inflammatory drug, Toradol. Average recovery time was an hour. I hope everyone had a designated driver to get there![8]

There are some weird cures around the world. In Ireland, they bury drunks up to their necks in moist river sand…the equivalent of a cold shower? In Puerto Rico, you rub the armpit of your drinking arm with a slice of lemon. If you get inebriated in Haiti, the voodoo cure choice is to stick 13 pins with black heads into the cork of the bottle you drank from. Wonder how they handle screw tops?

Smoothies are a great way to start your recovery process next morning. My personal favorite is the Breakfast Smoothie in Chapter 4. Bananas are a natural cure. The magnesium content relaxes the blood vessels that cause headaches and the iron fortifies the hemoglobin in the blood. Add honey and you'll build up the low blood sugar levels. Here's a smoothie that's good for you and your hangover.

---

8. www.businessweek.com/articles/2013-02-07/testing-the-hangover-cure-at-chicago-clinic-revive

GORDON'S HANGOVER SMOOTHIE

1 banana

1/3 cup strawberries

1 cup orange juice

3 teaspoons honey

Blend together with a few ice cubes

More combinations:

Add blueberries or raspberries

Add 1/2 cup yogurt

Add 1/2 cup milk

Okay guys, time to Party! Super Bowl®, March Madness, World Series, Olympics, Kentucky Derby, World Cup…whatever excuse you have to gather, now you can do it in a way that you can pig out and still not wreck your own body doing it!

NOTES:

CHAPTER 6

HELP! I'M HOME ALONE WITH THE KIDS!

When I was growing up, my three brothers and I would come home from school greeted by the most enticing smells permeating the whole the house: roasts in the oven, cookies baking and of course, my Georgia peach Mom's unbeatable Southern fried chicken. It's a great sense memory. The kitchen was a fascinating place and cooking seemed like magic as steaming pots on the stove turned into a delicious family meal around the table. I was a single father and my son Kalani was ten when he lived with me in an apartment behind my restaurant, The Basil Street Café. It was one of the first to feature a local, seasonal menu and organic food. Needless to say, we spent a lot of time together in the kitchen. As he grew, Kalani helped me with basic tasks, including clean up…cleanliness is essential in any cooking situation. Later, he went to culinary school and is a professional chef today.

Cooking is a great way to spend quality time with kids and teach them about food. The key is to think like them. Children are visual beings and if food looks appealing they're more likely to try it. If kids are picky eaters, make cooking an adventure. Let them help you plan the meal, choose recipes, make a list and shop. Take them to the farmers' market and let them pick fruits and vegetables. Kids that grow up in a city may never know that carrots have tops or Brussels sprouts grow on stalks until they visit those wonderful outdoor stalls. Add variety to your selections with things like kiwi, mango, papaya, snap peas, jicama…there are so many out-of-the-ordinary selections to choose from, you're sure to find some they like.

Supermarkets can also be a place to teach them about the power of what they put in their cart. Steer them away from the chips and candy aisles to the produce section. Some grocery chains even offer store tours with a nutritionist where kids learn about wholesome food choices, fun facts about fruits, veggies, whole grains and why breakfast is a very important meal. Dried fruits or nuts make a great alternative to junk food snacks. Rice cakes now come in flavors like apple cinnamon, caramel corn and chocolate crunch. Jamie Oliver, an English chef who started his American 'food revolution' seven years ago, believes schools should teach kids how to prepare nourishing meals and each student should graduate knowing ten recipes. This is a positive way to put them on the right food track for the future.

> **"Teaching kids how to feed themselves and how to live in a community responsibly is the center of an education."**
>
> —Alice Waters, chef, restaurateur, author, *The Edible Schoolyard*

After shopping, preparation can be a fun time. Read the recipe and the directions together, then see if the kids can repeat some of the ingredients. Ask them if they remember what to do first. Go through the utensils and explain what they're used for. This helps their listening skills and starts a conversation going about cooking. You may have various ages with you but even little ones can do simple things like tear lettuce, shuck corn, peel garlic or stir in spices. Teens can crack eggs, assemble ingredients and increase their math skills as they measure. Let them mix and whisk. Before they are allowed to chop, they must observe you. **Never** let kids use a knife without strict supervision. Best practice is to use a food processor to chop or dice. When you start cooking, remind children that stoves, ovens, pans and dishes can be very hot. Don't wear loose clothing that could catch fire. Tie their hair back so it doesn't get into food.

First things first. Kids need to know about kitchen safety and what they learn will last a lifetime. It will help avoid needless accidents but do keep emergency phone numbers posted in a visible place. This list looks like a lot to remember but these are the absolute basics needed to protect you and the kids:

- ✔ First rule, always wash your hands before cooking.
- ✔ Use supplies that won't break, like plastic measuring cups and stainless-steel bowls.
- ✔ Always check that appliances are switched to "off" before plugging in. Unplug them as soon as you finish using them.
- ✔ Turn pot handles to the back of the stove so they can't be knocked down or grabbed by little hands.
- ✔ Stir with wooden spoons because metal ones get hot.
- ✔ Use pot holders or oven mitts to grab handles. Never use a wet dish rag.

✔ When stirring on the stove, kids must be tall enough to see into the pot. Use a step stool if necessary.

✔ Always chop on a stable, non-slip surface. You can put a damp dish towel or rag under your cutting board to prevent shifting.

✔ Keep knives away from the edge of the counter where they can fall or be reached by children. Never try to catch a falling knife. EVER.

✔ Position oven racks before preheating the oven when they are cold.

✔ Clean up spills as soon as they happen.

✔ Keep a small fire extinguisher in the kitchen; know how to use it.

✔ Keep a first-aid kit handy and well stocked.

✔ Put a childproof lock on the cabinets with your cleaning supplies.

One more thing, make sure you have enough time in the kitchen with the kids. Don't try to squeeze in cooking a meal together after work or when you're on a schedule. A weekend when everyone is rested is a better time. It would be helpful if there were another adult on hand to keep an eye on things, especially if there are kids of different ages.

Now that you're well prepared. Here are a few simple recipes you can make together. Child obesity has become a national problem so to lower calories, use reduced fat or fat-free ingredients. Pizza is everyone's favorite and to make it quick and easy, use tortillas instead of dough. This recipe has multiple variations by changing the toppings. It's a great way to use leftovers and introduce kids to new tastes. Use all the toppings for "The Works" pizza.

EASY TORTILLA PIZZA

INGREDIENTS:

6 Large flour tortillas

1 48 oz jar pizza sauce

3 cups shredded mozzarella cheese

TOPPINGS:

Cooked, chopped chicken or turkey

Cooked, chopped ham

Pineapple

Chopped tomatoes

Roasted peppers

Meatballs (sliced)

Chopped bell peppers

Sliced olives

Chopped mushrooms

Chopped onions

Serves 6-8

DIRECTIONS:

1. Preheat Over to 400°.
2. Choose toppings and place in little bowls.
3. Arrange tortillas on a non-stick cookie sheet.
4. Spread a layer of pizza sauce on each one.
5. Add toppings.
6. Sprinkle with Mozzarella.
7. Bake until the cheese is melted and tortilla is crisp, about 10-15 minutes.

GORDON SAYS: *For a cool Italian variation kids will love, top with leftover pasta, like ziti or shells, then add more sauce and cheese. Try it!*

SOUTH OF THE BORDER PIZZA

INGREDIENTS:

4 flour tortillas

1 cup chopped, cooked chicken

2 tablespoons chicken stock

1 cup refried beans

1 cup chunky salsa

1 tablespoon taco seasoning mix

2 cups shredded Cheddar cheese

Serves 4-6

DIRECTIONS:

1. Preheat oven to 400°.
2. In a skillet or saucepan, Stir together the chicken, stock and taco seasoning. Cook over medium heat for 2 minutes.
3. Remove from the heat and set aside.
4. Arrange tortillas on a nonstick cookie sheet.
5. Top tortillas with beans, salsa, cheese and cooled chicken.
6. Bake until the cheese is melted and tortilla is crisp, about 10-15 minutes.

Bread is great way to introduce international food. There's pita bread from the Middle East, lavash from Armenia and Lebanon, naan from India, rye bread from Sweden, breadsticks from Italy and croissants from France. A fun thing to do would be to get a world map and mark the countries, then make sandwiches with one the those breads. Pita is one of the oldest known breads and this recipe uses the pocket style. So many people with busy schedules skip breakfast but it's not only an important meal to kick start your metabolism, it's a good way for the family to kick start the day.

BREAKFAST PITA POCKETS

INGREDIENTS:

2 pita pockets (cut in half)

6 eggs

4 slices bacon*

4 link sausages

Salt & Pepper to taste

Canadian Bacon or ham can be used.

Serves 4

DIRECTIONS:

1. Cook the bacon and sausages in a skillet over medium heat until browned.
2. Remove from heat and when cool, chop the sausage and crumble the bacon.
3. Beat eggs in a bowl.
4. Mix eggs, sausage and bacon in the skillet and cook until they are not runny.
5. Warm the pita in a toaster oven or microwave.
6. Spoon egg mixture into pita and serve.

Pancakes are a great breakfast for children of all ages. Ever wonder how they make those funny shapes? There are a few ways to do it. First you need batter! You can make your own with this simple recipe.

SCRATCH PANCAKES

INGREDIENTS:

1 cup flour

1 egg

1 teaspoon baking powder

1 teaspoon salt

1 cup milk

To sweeten the batter add:
- **1 teaspoon vanilla**
- **1 tablespoon sugar**

Makes about 12 small pancakes

DIRECTIONS:

1. Mix flour, egg, baking powder and salt
2. Gradually add milk and whisk till smooth
3. Spoon batter onto a hot greased griddle or a nonstick pan.
4. Wait till you see bubbles, then turn over and bake for another 2 minutes.
5. You can keep pancakes warm in the oven on a 250° setting.
6. Top with butter, maple syrup and a sprinkle of cinnamon.

GORDON'S TIP: *If the batter sits and gets thick, add a little milk. If it's too thin, add a little flour. Thinner batter and a cooler griddle will make thin pancakes.*

If you don't want to make your own batter, there are good mixes available. Some are even gluten-free, if that's an issue.

What about those funny shapes kids love? The simplest way to make them is to get a set of large cookie cutters or pancake molds. Silicon is better than metal because it has an easier release. A search for "pancake molds" on amazon.com will give you a wide variety of shapes: heroes and villains, Star Wars, flowers, bunnies, hearts, stars; Disney even sells a Mickey Mouse mold. If you want to make your own Mickey, just put two small pancakes for ears on the top sides of the large round one!

If you're using molds or cookie cutters, follow these directions:

- Fill a squeeze bottle with pancake batter.
- Place the molds on the grill or in a nonstick frying pan.
- Fill halfway with batter. (batter expands)
  If using metal, coat the cookie cutter inside with nonstick spray.
- When the batter bubbles, flip it over. Push down a little.
- Remove the mold and slide out the pancakes.

If you're feeling creative, here's another way you can make shapes just using the squeeze bottle. Make an outline with the batter, wait a few minutes, then fill it in and cook until you see the bubbles. Flip and cook another 2 minutes.

For simple round pancakes, get the kids involved in decorating. You can make faces with fruit, blueberries for eyes, whipped cream for a mouth, cut strawberry eyebrows. Something that always brings back memories of my childhood is peanut butter and jelly. Here is a fun French toast recipe to satisfy that craving.

PEANUT BUTTER STUFFED FRENCH TOAST

INGREDIENTS:

1/4 cup milk

4 eggs

1-1/2 teaspoons vanilla extract

Creamy peanut butter

8 bread slices (medium thick)

2 tablespoons butter

Serve with maple syrup.

DIRECTIONS:

1. In a flat baking dish, whisk the milk, eggs and vanilla.
2. Spread a thin layer of peanut butter on the bottom half of 4 bread slices
3. Place remaining slices on top.
4. Dip each side in the egg mixture but don't make it too soggy.
5. Heat butter in the skillet (don't burn it).
6. Add egg sandwiches to skillet and cook to golden brown, about 2 minutes on each side.

Serves 4; cut in 1/2 for kids

GORDON SAYS: *Vary this French toast recipe by adding jams and fruit or substituting cream cheese for the peanut butter.*

"Peanut butter is the paté of childhood."

—Florence Fabricant, food writer, the *New York Times*

Kids don't always want to eat eggs. Here's a breakfast that looks like a pizza and they can have fun assembling.

MORNING EGG PIZZAS

INGREDIENTS:

4 English muffins

1 large tomato, (4 slices)

2 hard boiled eggs, peeled and sliced in half

Shredded mozzarella cheese

Olive oil or butter

Serves 4-8 kids

DIRECTIONS:

1. Toast the English muffins.
2. Put them on a cookie sheet.
3. Drizzle with olive oil or you can butter them.
4. Layer tomato, an egg slice, yoke down, on each half.
5. Salt and pepper to taste.
6. Sprinkle with mozzarella.
7. Broil 5 minutes or until cheese melts.

GORDON'S WARNING: *Most toaster ovens have a broiler but some ovens are small, so be careful that the food doesn't touch the top heating element.*

Hate that ring around the green yoke in hard boiled eggs? Here's the way you can get that perfect golden color every time.

THE PERFECT HARD BOILED EGG

1. Place the eggs in a single layer in a saucepan and completely cover with cold water.
2. Add 2 tablespoons of white vinegar to the water so the shells won't crack.
3. Bring the water to a boil and turn off the heat.
4. Cover the pot for 15 minutes (no longer).
5. Drain and rinse with cold water.

Guys, don't get lazy and serve those sugar-laden cereals that have no redeeming nutritional value. Make the effort. Keep them cooking.

> **"Breakfast cereals that come in the same colors as polyester leisure suits make oversleeping a pleasure."**
>
> —Fran Lebowitz, American author *Metropolitan Life*

This next recipe is a fun morning dish or a late family supper. Eggs give it a high protein boost. The kids will love crunching up those chips.

TORTILLA CHIP SCRAMBLE

INGREDIENTS:

- 1 cup tortilla chips, crushed
- 3/4 cup red mild salsa (drained)
- 10 eggs
- 1/4 cup milk
- 1 cup shredded Monterey Jack or Cheddar cheese (or 1/2 cup each)
- 1-1/2 tablespoons butter
- Salt and pepper to taste

DIRECTIONS:

1. In a bowl, whisk together the eggs, milk, salt and pepper.
2. Heat the butter in a frying pan over medium heat (don't burn it!)
3. Pour the egg mixture into the pan and stir as it cooks until almost set (about 3 minutes).
4. Add the cheese and when it melts remove from heat.
5. Stir in the chips.

Serves 6

Casseroles are a good one dish lunch or dinner. This one is great because it's a healthy alternative to the traditional beef nacho casserole. Kids will love it.

NACHO CASSEROLE

INGREDIENTS:

1 lb ground turkey

1 can whole kernel corn (drained)

3/4 cup sour cream

2 cups shredded Cheddar cheese

1-1/2 cups salsa

About 25 tortilla chips, crushed

1/4 teaspoon salt

Pepper to taste

Serves 6

DIRECTIONS:

1. Preheat over to 350°.
2. Place turkey in a skillet and cook, crumbling with a fork until brown.
3. Remove from heat. Drain grease.
4. Stir in corn, sour cream, salsa, salt and pepper.
5. In a casserole, layer the turkey mixture, then the chips and a layer of cheese. Repeat ending with the cheese.
6. Bake uncovered until cheese is melted and dish is heated through, about 20 minutes.

Here is a recipe for hamburgers that sounds simple, but just adding the sautéed onions and that hint of spice makes a world of difference in the flavor even the kids will love.

GORDON'S HAMBURGERS

INGREDIENTS:

1 lb hamburger meat (85% lean)

1 large onion

1 tablespoon olive oil

1 tablespoon Cajun spice

Sliced cheddar cheese

Serves 6

DIRECTIONS:

1. Chop the onion and sauté in the oil.
2. When the onions turn transparent, add the Cajun spice and sauté for 2 minutes more.
3. Remove from pan and set aside to cool.
4. When cool, mix well with hamburger meat.
5. Make patties and grill in a skillet. Top will cheese and cover until melted

> "I still love making hamburgers…whenever I eat them childhood memories come up for me."
>
> —Bobby Flay, American chef, writer and restaurateur

Hamburgers are an easy lunch, but I remember how my brothers and I used to love it when Mom would make Sloppy Joe's. This is a simple one you and the kids can make.

SIMPLE SLOPPY JOES

INGREDIENTS:

- 1-1/2 lbs ground beef or ground turkey
- 1 small onion, chopped
- 1 cup ketchup
- 2 teaspoons white vinegar
- 2 tablespoons brown sugar
- 2 tablespoons yellow mustard
- Salt and pepper to taste

DIRECTIONS:

1. Combine ketchup, vinegar, sugar, mustard, salt and pepper in a small bowl and mix. Set aside.
2. In a skillet, cook the onions with medium heat about 2 minutes.
3. Add meat and crumble it with a fork until is fully cooked. Drain fat.
4. Stir the ketchup mixture with the meat and cook 10 minutes over medium-low heat.
5. Serve on small hamburger buns.

Serves 4-6

> "Man who invented the hamburger was smart; man who invented the cheeseburger was a genius."
>
> —Matthew McConaughey, American Actor

When you go to the store you will see various tortilla sizes. For a burrito or these chimichangas you need to allow room for the filling. I'd use an 8" round for a child portion size. You'll have fun assembling these. Kids love roll ups!

CHEESY CHIMICHANGAS

INGREDIENTS:

4 large flour tortillas 8"-12" diameter

1 can refried beans

8 oz shredded cheddar or jack cheese

1 cup cooked shredded chicken

1/4 cup chopped green onions

Lettuce

Tomato

cooking spray

Toppings: Salsa, Sour cream, Guacamole

Serves 4-6

DIRECTIONS:

1. Spread the tortillas out flat. Add filling down the center about 4" wide. Leave 3" at the bottom and top for fold.
2. Spread 1/4 cup of beans down the center of the tortilla.
3. Add chicken cheese, lettuce and tomato to the bean layer. About 2 tablespoons each.
4. Fold like a burrito, bottom end up first, then fold in the sides and close top.
5. Place seam sides down in a 15" x 10" x 1" baking pan coated with cooking spray. Brush with butter.
6. Bake, uncovered, at 375° for 20-25 minutes or until heated through.

GORDON'S TIP: *To keep the filling from falling out, mix 1/4 cup flour and 1/2 cup warm water to make a creamy paste. Spread this on the outer edges of the tortilla when you fold it. This will seal the burrito.*

When I was raising my son, my twin brother Greg had two girls. His wife Diane came up with this dish which was one of their favorites. If you have nothing in the house, you can usually dig up these three ingredients for a quick and easy dish.

TUNA PATTIES / SLIDERS

INGREDIENTS:

2 cans tuna, drained*

2 eggs, lightly beaten

1/2 cup breadcrumbs

1/4 teaspoon salt, pepper

Can substitute ground beef for tuna.

Serves 4

DIRECTIONS:

1. Mix the tuna with the beaten eggs and breadcrumbs.
2. Season with salt and pepper.
3. Shape into 4 large patties. Make smaller patties for sliders.
4. Fry in a skillet over medium heat, 3 minutes on each side.
5. Serve on a hamburger bun with condiments including ketchup, relish, lettuce, tomato. For a crunch, top with potato chips or fried onions.

Kids go crazy over chicken nuggets, also called chicken fingers, and all the fast food restaurants make them. You can make them too, but these are healthier because they're baked and not fried.

CHICKEN FINGERS

INGREDIENTS:

2 boneless chicken breasts cut into strips or bite-sized pieces

1 cup Italian seasoned breadcrumbs

2 eggs*

1/4 cup milk*

Salt and pepper to taste

Substitute ranch dressing for the egg-milk mixture for a zesty variation.

Serves 4-6

DIRECTIONS:

1. Preheat oven to 350°.
2. Mix the eggs, milk, salt and pepper.
3. Roll the chicken pieces in the egg mixture, then roll in the bread crumbs.
4. Arrange on a cookie sheet.
5. Bake for 10 minutes and then turn them over.
6. Cook 10 more minutes until they are brown and pierce easily with a fork.

Don't forget dessert. Another one from Diane's kitchen is this fruit and pudding cake the kids all asked for on their birthdays. Quick, easy and no oven is involved!

NO BAKE CAKE

INGREDIENTS:

Pound cake cut into 1/2 slices

1 cup sliced strawberries (no tops)

1 cup sliced bananas

1 cup blueberries

Prepared vanilla pudding

Whipped cream

Serves 6-8

DIRECTIONS:

1. In a 9" x 12" glass baking dish, make a layer of pound cake.
2. Next, layer the pudding, bananas, blueberries and strawberries.
3. Repeat, ending with strawberries.
4. Top with a layer of whipped cream.
5. Cut and serve.

I try to stay away from sugar in dessert recipes. These are yogurt based.

AMAZING AMBROSIA

INGREDIENTS:

1 cup mini marshmallows

8 oz can crushed pineapple, drained

11 oz can mandarin oranges drained

1/2 cup shredded sweetened coconut

3/4 cup vanilla yogurt

Cool Whip

Serves 4-6

DIRECTIONS:

1. Gently mix yogurt into the fruit.
2. Refrigerate 1 hour. Stir before serving.
3. Top with Cool Whip.

FOOL PROOF PARFAIT

INGREDIENTS:

2 cups vanilla yogurt

1 cups bananas, sliced

1 cup fresh strawberries, sliced (can use thawed frozen thawed)

2 teaspoons sugar

1 cup graham crackers, crumbled

Whipped cream topping (optional)

Serves 4-6

DIRECTIONS:

1. Mix the strawberries and sugar together.
2. Spoon 1 tablespoon of yogurt into the bottom of a sturdy 6-8 oz glass. Layer with sliced bananas, sliced strawberries and crumbled graham crackers.
3. Repeat the layers to the top of the glass.
4. Top with whipped cream for pizzazz.
5. Cover each glass with plastic wrap and chill for up to 2 hours before serving.

Here are the instructions for a bunny cake my niece Heather made. It's easy and fun to do. You need two 9" round cake pans. Use a packaged cake mix and white frosting sprinkled with coconut. Decorate with licorice and jelly beans, flowers, candy…let the kids get creative!

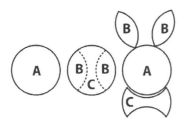

Heather made these snow bunnies with cupcakes, jelly beans, marshmallows, pink sprinkles, Twizzlers and candy eggs! Check out www.cakeshapesdesigns.com, a site that offers a wide variety of downloadable patterns for a fee around $5.00 each.

FINAL THOUGHTS

You have to relax when you're cooking with kids in the kitchen. They might make a mess and spill things. They might even break things. Mistakes don't count because you want the kids to be there. A negative reaction could affect them for their whole life because all they might remember is that the kitchen is a place where people get angry. It's really is a place you can play and bond and have fun with your kids.

> **"The kitchen really is the castle itself. This is where we spend our happiest moments and where we find the joy of being a family."**
> —Mario Batali, American chef, writer and restaurateur

NOTES:

CHAPTER 7
RESCUE REMEDIES

WHAT TO DO WHEN THINGS GO WRONG...
AND OTHER GOOD STUFF TO KNOW

I mentioned before that even as a chef I've had my share of cooking fiascos. Our unspoken kitchen crew motto is: "No matter what happens, never let them see it out front." Since this is a survival guide, it's important to talk about what to do when you screw up 'cause no matter how carefully you follow a recipe, a thousand things can happen. Your favorite team makes a touchdown in the last three seconds to win the game. You got absorbed and the baked beans burned. Your girlfriend calls. You already put salt in the soup but forgot, so you salt it again making a liquid you could float on. The uncut DVD of your favorite film has additional scenes. You timed your chili for the theatrical version and it now resembles a lunar landscape. Your roast was ready at seven and your guests arrive at eight making the meat suitable for shoes. Never fear. Chef Gordon is here. All is not lost. An athlete in a slump doesn't give up; it doesn't mean he can't cut it. So it goes in the kitchen. A burned meatloaf doesn't mean you can't cook. While I can't cover all of the things that might happen, I think these are the most common ones. I also included what people ask me over and over again when food is too spicy, overcooked, undercooked, peppery, burned, shriveled, mushy, curdled, greasy…you get the picture. Don't throw in the dish towel. Your next call doesn't have to be for reservations. Even the best chefs have things go wrong. Here are a few simple remedies.

You'll need some EMERGENCY BASICS for your kitchen 'first aid' cabinet.

1. Sugar
2. Lemons
3. Cooking sherry
4. Cornstarch
5. White vinegar
6. Potatoes
7. Potato flakes

"Pepper is small in quantity and great in virtue."

—Plato, Greek philosopher (570-495 BC)

"Salt is born of the purest of parents: the sun and the sea."

—Pythagoras, Greek philosopher (580-500 BC)

Salt and pepper are great seasonings. Salt has been used to preserve meat almost since the time man began to hunt. It also helps your body regulate its fluid balance. Because salt and pepper enhance flavor, it's better to add them while cooking rather than sprinkling them on food afterwards. Too much salt or pepper can overpower a dish. Here's what you can do if you got heavy-handed or absent minded.

Too Salty Soup or Stew: The remedy I've heard suggested most often is to throw in large potato chunks or slices and let them simmer for 10-15 minutes. When you fish out the pieces, supposedly the potatoes have absorbed a lot of the salt. However, my go-to book for kitchen science is *What Einstein Told His Cook*, by Robert Wolke. He performed a controlled experiment and found out that, while the potatoes absorbed salt water, they actually did not change the taste of the liquid. Some other touted options are to add lemon juice, sugar and vinegar, but the only proven way to rescue over-salted soup or stew is to add more liquid. Be sure it's unsalted!

GORDON'S WARNING: *Never measure seasonings right over the pot or bowl. It's too easy for your hand to slip if the dog jumps on your leg or your girlfriend tries something naughty while you're cooking.*

Too Much Pepper – Too Spicy: The way you can turn down the heat is to add sugar and if possible, add more of the other ingredients. The Scoville scale which measures the heat of peppers was developed by adding a sugar solution to peppers until the heat was neutralized.[1] On this scale, green pepper registers zero. For hot chili, add a small can of crushed pineapple. It will dissolve and counteract the heat. For salsa, squirt in some lime. Canned corn can also work to tame out-of-control heat or pepper.

Burned Beyond Saving? If your food is burning, don't call Ladder 16, there are things you can do to rescue it.

1. Immediately remove the pan from the heat to stop cooking.
2. Run cold water over the pot bottom or immerse in a pan of cold water.
3. Transfer the unburned portion to a clean pot. If the top layer tastes okay, immediately pour the top half of the liquid into another container. Taste again.
4. If no burned taste is in the bottom half of the pot, pour that into your container, leaving the bottom inch or so in the original pot. DO NOT STIR OR SCRAPE the bottom of the pot.

---

1. www.chilliworld.com/factfile/scoville_scale.asp

If it's only slightly burned, try adding some milk but remember, a scorched taste overpowers flavor. You can call it smoky, country-style or blackened, but sometimes burned food is too far gone to save and needs to be trashed. In that case, start over, order a pizza or make a reservation.

If You Have Set Your Food On Fire: Unless you're trying to flambé, throw on some baking soda. It's a natural extinguisher for grease fires.

Can You Clean A Burned Pot? Yes, I've been there and you can. If you have food burned into the bottom this works for me:

1. Cover the burnt part with 1 cup of white vinegar and 1 cup of water (or more depending on the size). Boil it.
2. Remove the pan from the heat and add 2 tablespoons of baking soda. It will fizz.
3. Empty the pan and when cool, scrub with a scouring pad.

Nonstick Pans: Sprinkle baking soda on it and then spray with white vinegar. Let it soak. If the baking soda hardens, just spray with vinegar again. Scour with a plastic pad.

GORDON'S WARNING: *Nonstick pans should be thrown out if very overheated. Never use metal utensils on nonstick cookware because it can scrape off the coating. If they are badly scratched, get rid of them!*

How to Repair Food by John and Marina Bear is a great comprehensive guide to fixing kitchen mistakes. *Oops* by Cooking Light has 209 Solutions for everyday kitchen mistakes. Check them out.

WILTED VEGGIES

If they're not stored properly, veggies can get limp faster than a guy looking at his judgmental mother-in-law! You can reinvigorate them with a few simple tricks.

Celery: Cut off the bottom, stick the stalks in ice water for 2-3 hours. Add a tablespoon of white vinegar and celery will be as crunchy as ever.

Carrots: Do the same thing you did for the celery. Keep carrots fresh by cleaning them under running water with a scrub brush and dry them with a paper towel. Store them in a zip lock bag. They'll be good for up to 2 weeks.

Lettuce: For leafy greens, plop them in ice water with a tablespoon or two of vinegar for eight to ten minutes. This will give them back their crunch.

GORDON SAYS: *If vegetables are wet when you put them away, they're more susceptible to bacterial growth. Wash them just before you're ready to use them.*

Dried Out Bread: To revive it, give the bread a quick, light spray of water before placing it in a preheated 350° oven or toaster oven for 5-7 minutes. Bread will crisp right up but eat it within an hour or two.

GORDON'S WARNING: *Don't keep stirring rice during cooking. This breaks down the grain and you'll get a starchy sticky mess. Don't lift the cover! It stops the cooking process.*

Overcooked Roast: It may look like it's ready for jerky, but you can revive a dried-out roast to something edible in only a few minutes.

1. Cut the meat against the grain into slices as thin as possible.
2. Arrange the slices in a casserole dish.
3. Transfer any roast pan drippings to a saucepan and add 2 cups of

chicken, beef or vegetable stock. Bring the mixture to a boil and remove it from the heat.

4. Pour the mixture over the meat slices in the casserole dish.
5. Cover the dish with foil and place into pre-heated 250° to 300° oven for five to ten minutes.
6. Taste the meat to ensure that it is more juicy and tender before serving; otherwise, allow the meat to absorb the liquid for a few more minutes. Call it country-style.

> **"The only real stumbling block is fear of failure. In cooking you've got to have a what-the-hell attitude."**
>
> —Julia Child, chef, TV personality, author

TRICKS OF THE TRADE

Stop Bacon from Curling: Bake it at 400° for 10-15 minutes, it tastes the same but stays flat.

Bacon Slices Stick Together: Roll up the entire package lengthwise and the strips will separate. Store rolled up with a rubber band around it.

Burned Butter: When you see butter is browning too fast, add a little oil (any kind except motor). If badly burned, toss it and start over.

Overcooked Veggies: If you have killed carrots, sweet potatoes, peas or most any other vegetable way past the point of doneness, never fear, purée is here. Dump the veggies in the food processor or blender with a little cream and butter. This is an impressive whipped side dish that makes you look like a true gourmet cook. Add chicken stock and more cream to turn it into a fancy soup.

Lumpy Sauce: Remove the liquid from the pan and beat it with a whisk or in the food processor or blender. Serve on the side or pour over the dish. No one will be the wiser.

Gravy Too Bland: Strain the juice of whatever meat you cook, add stock or bouillon cubes or, for a great flavor, add cooking sherry and boil it off. For chicken, add some bouillon cubes or granules.

Gravy Too Thin: You can thicken it with these: *Wondra* – I like it is best because it doesn't get lumpy; *Corn starch* – add about 1-1/12 teaspoons per cup. Allow the gravy to cook so you don't get a starchy taste; *Mashed potato flakes* – another handy thickener to have around; *Arrowroot* – add one tablespoon per cup of liquid. You can add just before serving because it has no taste. *Flour and water* – making a smooth paste is tricky and the last thing I'd suggest!

Burned Rice: You thought you had to cook it for hours didn't you? To get the scorched taste out, place a slice of bread over the rice and cover the pot for 10 minutes. That should help. Don't scrape the bottom part from the pot! Toss with a few lumps of butter and serve.

Runny Mashed Potatoes: Add potato flakes or powdered milk.

Ketchup Krisis! That exasperating ketchup problem. When it won't pour, don't physically abuse the bottle. One way to get it flowing is to stick a soda straw into the bottle. That passes enough air through for the liquid to come out easily. The scientists at Heinz actually did a study and here's what they found. To release ketchup faster from the glass bottle, apply a firm tap to the sweet spot on the neck of the bottle— the "57." A secret straight from the ketchup-makers mouth!

Onions: Real cooks don't cry. To avoid weeping, peel under cold water or, if you have time, put onions in the freezer for 10-15 minutes before cutting.

INCREDIBLE EDIBLE EGGS

Hard Boiled Eggs Won't Crack or Peel: Put the eggs in a bowl of cold water and tap the shells. This will make a slight crack so water can seep in and loosen the shell, making it easy to peel.

Eggs Crack During Cooking: Put a teaspoon of salt or a few drops of lemon juice into the water. Add vinegar to the water when boiling eggs; it helps seal the shell.

Poached Eggs Get Runny: Put a few drops of vinegar into the water.

Fresh, Rotten or Hard Boiled? If you can't remember if an egg is fresh or hard boiled, spin the egg. If it wobbles, it's raw. If it spins easily, it's hard boiled. A fresh egg will sink in water, a cooked one will float.

A Fluffy Scramble: For light, fluffy scrambled eggs, add a little water or milk while beating the eggs.[2]

> "One of the most private things in the world is an egg before it is broken."
> —M.F.K. Fisher, American food writer, *The Art of Eating*

OTHER GOOD STUFF TO KNOW

Tomatoes: Keep them at room temperature and out of direct sunlight. They'll keep for three to four days. A sliced tomato can be kept wrapped in plastic in the fridge for just a few days.

Mold: Maybe they discovered penicillin this way but your refrigerator is not a science lab. Some mold can cause food-borne illness but not all food is ruined with a patch of mold. You can cut away the green part of cheese (unless it's on Roquefort or Gorgonzola which is part of the flavor.) Furry berries should be tossed along with those that were in direct contact them. If something looks like toxic waste, throw it out or feed to the Incredible Hulk.

---

2. Eggheads should check out Michel Roux's book *Eggs* for more tips.

Fishy Fish: Thaw fish in milk. This gives it a fresh taste.

Pasta Sticks Together: After cooking, sauce pasta immediately or toss with some olive oil. If it's stuck together in a ball, put it back in some boiling water for a few minutes to separate it. For large noodles, like lasagna, put a tablespoon of oil in the water so they won't stick together while cooking.

Boiling Over Pot: To stop water from boiling over, coat the top 1" of the pot with oil, but don't overfill it in the first place.

Remove Fat From Soups and Stews. Wrap a few ice cubes in a paper towel or cheesecloth and skim over the top of the pot. The fat will cling to the cubes as you stir. Fat also clings to lettuce leaves.

Hard Sugar: Your box of sugar has turned into a weapon. You can break up a hardened lump by: 1) putting it in a food processor or blender; 2) putting in it a plastic bag and steaming it ; 3) smashing it with a hammer (last one feels the best).

How to Open a Coconut: One hard job made easier. Poke a hole in each end with a hammer and large screw driver or corkscrew to enlarge the holes (or you'll make a bomb!) Drain out the milk. If it smells sweet it's ok to eat. Cook for 20-25 minutes in a preheated 300° oven or until you hear a pop and it has cracked. Remove and hit the shell with a hammer until it splits. The meat will fall away from the shell. Yum!

When Is Pineapple Ripe? When you can easily pull a leaf from the center.

How to Pick an Eggplant: It should be not too big and not too dark. That means it's older with more seeds and can be bitter. Flesh should give slightly and spring back. If it's hard, it's not ripe enough.

GORDON SAYS: *Sprinkle sliced, peeled eggplant with salt and let it sit for 10 minutes to help reduce bitterness and firm up the flesh; it's easier to cook.*

My Power Went Out: Can I refreeze my food? Yes, if it's still icy or very cold. Thawed food can grow bacteria and freezing doesn't kill it. Better to cook the food and then freeze it. If you have time, the best way to thaw food is in the refrigerator.

Honey Crystallizes: Put the jar in a pan of hot water.

Too Many Lemons: Squeeze the juice and freeze it ice cube trays.

Carving Meat: Don't cut it straight from the oven. Hot slicing releases the juices; letting it rest distributes them more evenly inside. Wait 20-30 minutes before carving turkeys or large roasts.

Blending: When processing in a blender, be sure the lid is on tight and don't fill the container more than half-way unless you want to decorate your ceiling.

Knives: Cut away from your body when using a knife. Clean handles to avoid slipping. Don't toss knives in a sink of soapy water where you can't see them.

Appliances: Throw out any appliance that's damaged. New ones are fairly inexpensive. Check out thrift stores. They usually test appliances before sale but be sure it works before you buy it. I've even found new appliances there.

Toaster: Would you be shocked to know you should never stick a fork in a toaster to retrieve anything trapped there? You will be shocked if you do that!

Pot Lids: Be careful lifting lids when you're cooking. Oh, and don't forget to use a potholder! Hot steam can scald you. Watch out when you open that hot bag of microwave popcorn too. Been there…done that!

Funky Sponges: Pee whew! That awful smell comes from bacteria. The dampness is an ideal breeding ground for germs. Two minutes in the microwave at full power kills disease causing spores, including E. coli. You can also soak sponges in bleach.

Last but not least, when you shout FIRE, here's what to do:

Fire in the Microwave: Yep, it happens. Turn the microwave off and keep the door closed. Fire can't burn without oxygen.

Fire on the Stove Top: Put a lid on the pot, turn off the burner, grab a potholder and move the pan to a cool burner, or remove it from the stove. Don't put it on a surface where it will leave burned spot!

Fire in the Oven: Leave the oven door closed! Remember, oxygen feeds the flames. Turn off the oven and let the fire burn itself out. If it continues to burn, call 911.

Grease Fire: Never douse it with water. Baking soda works but will only extinguish a small fire. Don't throw flour on it. One cup creates the explosive force of two sticks of dynamite. If you have a fire extinguisher, make sure you know how to use it. Aim at the base of the fire—not the flames.

GORDON'S WARNING: *When oil heats, first it boils, then starts smoking and then catches on fire. Grease fires are liquid and can spread quickly. If you can't control the flames, get out of Dodge and call the fire department!*

"In the abstract art of cooking, ingredients trump appliances, passion supersedes expertise, creativity triumphs over technique, spontaneity inspires invention, and wine makes even the worst culinary disaster taste delicious."

—Bob Blumer, author and host of *The Surreal Gourmet*

THINGS YOUR FATHER NEVER TOLD YOU

Here are some useful bits of information anyone can use. Stains are a big problem and not just in the kitchen. Before you try any remedy, check the fabric to be sure it's washable. When in doubt, dry clean it. Getting cold water on a stain right away is recommended. Stains are harder to remove when they dry. Dabbing with club soda will keep a stain from setting. Here are some common removal tips.

Wine: Dried wine stains can be removed by soaking in equal parts of hydrogen peroxide and liquid dish soap. Rub the mixture into the stain; let it sit for about 30 minutes. Rinse with warm water.

Blood: Run the stain under cold water; hot water will set it. Mix 1/2 teaspoon of liquid dish washing detergent, 1 tablespoon of ammonia and 1 quart of cool water in a basin and soak. Let it sit for 15 minutes, then rinse.

Chocolate: Soak in cold water. Bleach with hydrogen peroxide. Wet the stain and then add a drop or two of ammonia. Let it sit for a few minutes, then rinse.

Coffee: If you can't put cold water on it right away, soak in a solution of 1 part white vinegar to 2 parts water. Rinse with cold water.

Gravy: If it's fresh, put salt on the stain to absorb the grease and gently brush it off. If it's already dry, try the white vinegar and water solution.

Lipstick: Don't go out with painted women! Seriously, if you have a lipstick stain, try OxiClean. It works on most grease stains. You can also try rubbing non-gel toothpaste into the stain, then launder as usual.

Dull Scissors: Cut 150 grit sandpaper or folded aluminum foil to sharpen the blades.

Burns: Don't butter them! This is an old wives' tale. To draw out the heat, run the burned area under cold water. Never put ice on a burn. Aloe Vera can soothe and help heal it. Don't use any tight covering. My own proven pain remedy…two shots of Tequila!

Cuts: I've had a few scars over the years. If you get a gusher, put some pepper on it to coagulate the blood, then cover with a band-aid and a rubber fingertip.

Smelly Hands: Wash them in cold water and rub with salt. Rub with a raw unpeeled potato. You can get rid of that fishy smell by rubbing your hands with salt and then lemon rind. Also, try washing your hands with toothpaste.

Cutting English Muffins: Don't use a knife to cut them cause you'll flatten those yummy nooks and crannies. Use a fork to separate them.

Glasses Stuck Together: That's so annoying! They'll come apart if you put cold water in the top one and put the bottom one in hot water.

Now, take a glass, pour yourself a cold one and watch some football. You've earned it!

NOTES:

CHAPTER 8

OTHER FOOD FOR THOUGHT

GROW YOUR OWN

Whatever you think this means, I'm talking about food! I'm sure you're thinking a garden requires space, soil and back-breaking work. Forget all that. Sure, you can use that conventional method, but I'm going to show you how you can grow a bounty of fruits and vegetables almost anywhere, from an apartment terrace to your garage roof! You don't need a green thumb…you don't even need any dirt! It's called "vertical growing."

I began investigating this system when my urban friends started looking for relief from rising grocery store prices. Produce can vary from week to week as overhead rises. Whatever the cost, even from a local farmers' market, home food production is less expensive. Seeds can be purchased online or from nurseries where you can also purchase pre-sprouted plants for just a few dollars more. You can buy 900 seeds for around $2.00. Think of how many heads of lettuce that will grow!

As city life exploded, consumers became more distant from their food sources. On average, major cities import 6,000 tons of food each day, with an average distance of 1,700 miles from farm to table. Growing your own food not only reduces food cost, it increases food quality.

So how does it work without dirt? Vertical growing containers use a soil substitute which allows more control over plant nutrition. This mix is a natural growing media of coconut fiber and perlite which is clean and porous. These materials enhance nutrient delivery, improving plant growth, roots, bloom, yield and defend plants from disease. The vertical growing unit is completely self-contained and can include an automated watering system. Water is a critical issue in many areas since food production uses a major percentage of those resources. Vertical growing saves, on an average, 75% of the water used in traditional farming.

The reason plants stop producing in soil is not air temperature, but rather, soil temperature. The stackable pots are insulated to protect the plants and roots from both cold and heat. It is possible to have high quality fruits and vegetables year round but you do need sun and it can't be freezing cold.

The vertical growing system is designed for simplicity. It can be set up in any flat area and the lightweight, stackable pots are very easy to move. Since the majority of fertilizers and pesticides are made from petroleum products, vertical growing can decrease the carbon footprint. In a home with a yard or a large space, a cornucopia of fruits and vegetables

Four single stacks grow strawberries on the side of my house in Los Angeles.

GORDON SAYS: *Did you know that cities cover only 2% of the earth's surface but consume 75% of its resources? More and more metropolitan dwellers are turning "green."*

can be grown including lettuce, tomatoes, strawberries, peppers, broccoli, greens, eggplants parsley, basil, herbs and even flowers. The stackable pots are insulated to protect the plants from extreme temperatures.

Vertical growing in your own home gives new meaning to "locally grown" and "organic." There are lots of different types of systems. Google "vertical growing" to find one in your area.

(Above, left) We have fresh strawberries year round for my smoothies. (Center) A tower with rocket arugula and basil. (Right) My Fall lettuce crop.

WHAT THE HECK IS ORGANIC?

The term "organic" has been thrown around a lot and appears on everything from food to cosmetics and beer. But how do you know if something is really organic? There are some very clear guidelines. Simply stated, organic produce and other ingredients are grown without the use of pesticides, synthetic fertilizers, sewage sludge, genetically modified organisms or ionizing radiation.

The United States Department of Agriculture (USDA) decides which foods can be considered organic. This means that food products, whether meat, vegetable, fruit or dairy, are not organic unless they have been certified by the USDA and bear the USDA stamp of approval. If you're not certified, you can't make any organic claim on the principal display panel or use that USDA organic seal anywhere on the package. You can only identify the certified organic ingredients as organic and the percentage of organic ingredients.

The USDA has three categories of labeling for organic products:

- **100% Organic:** Made with 100% organic ingredients; all ingredients must be certified organic and any processing aids must be organic. Product labels must state the name of the certifying agent on the information panel.
- **Organic:** Made with at least 95% organic ingredients.
- **Made With Organic Ingredients:** Made with a minimum of 70% organic ingredients with strict restrictions on the remaining 30% including no GMOs (genetically modified organisms).

Products with less than 70% organic ingredients may list organically produced ingredients on the side panel of the package, but may not make any organic claims on the front of the package.

The philosophy of organic livestock production is to provide conditions that meet the health needs and natural behavior of the animal: access to the outdoors, fresh air, water, sunshine and pasture. Organic livestock must be fed 100% organic feed, free of any animal by-products, hormones, antibiotics or other drugs. If an organic animal gets sick and is given antibiotics, its meat, milk or eggs cannot be marketed as organic. Did you know that certified organic farmers must keep extensive records to trace the animal from birth to the market?

Now let's talk about those three controversial letters, GMO. What is it? Why is it bad for you? Is it really that bad? Let's take a look. "Genetically Modified Organism," refers to a living organism whose genes have been altered by the changing or relocating of living cells. This is called "transgenic" technology. In crops, it's been used to enhance resistance to insecticides, herbicides or pesticides, increase drought tolerance, encourage higher yields or promote the ability to plant more in a smaller area. Today, over 90% of US corn and cotton crops are genetically modified. News flash for those soy militants who won't drink milk and are radical about soy-based products—90% of those little beans are genetically modified. GM sugar beets were introduced in 2008, and today, 90% of those grown in the U.S. are genetically modified. Sugar not made from cane is likely made from sugar beets.

So what's the problem? There are two major issues: Genetically Modified (GM) foods may contain antibiotic-resistant genes that could pick up bacteria, which in turn may infect us, and those altered foods may contain unseen and unknown food allergens. The long-term effects of GMOs on human body processes are unknown. Some scientists believe gene splicing provides the opportunity for new combinations of genes to trigger allergic reactions. While some U.S. farmers have embraced GM seeds, advocacy groups are alarmed that they have travelled a slippery slope where it's possible some mistakes can't be corrected. Big agri-business companies like Monsanto claim that their goal is to end world hunger, but most of their investment has been in for-profit crop research. Because organic farmers are required to meet rigorous audit requirements, we know that those farmers have not used GMOs, and have taken all required measures to protect against contamination.

The most common "Frankenfoods" are those that contain Genetically Modified ingredients: baked goods, pancakes, bread and even gravies. Other top offenders are corn, canola and cottonseed oil, definitely not as pure as they used to be. Since right now we don't have required GMO labeling, the best thing to do is buy organic. So…

LET'S GET BACK TO ORGANICS

If your budget is limited (and whose isn't these days), the best bang for your organic buck is produce. But here's the thing. Some produce is more susceptible to pesticides than others. This list has the "Dirty Dozen" on the left, and the "Not-So-Dirty" on the right.[1]

More Susceptible to Pesticide	Less Susceptible to Pesticide
Peaches	Papayas
Apples	Broccoli
Sweet bell peppers	Cabbage
Celery	Bananas
Nectarines	Kiwi
Strawberries	Sweet peas (frozen)
Cherries	Asparagus
Pears	Mangoes
Grapes (imported)	Pineapple
Spinach	Sweet corn (frozen)
Lettuce	Avocados
Potatoes	Onions

Whether your produce is organic or not, you should always:
- Wash produce, especially with edible skin. Never use soap. You can buy a veggie wash at Whole Foods or a health food store.
- Remove the peel from fruits and vegetables.
- Discard the outer leaves of leafy vegetables.
- Toss any cut produce that's been left out four hours or more.

Also, trim the visible fat and skin from meat and poultry since pesticide residues can live in there.

---

1. Organics: Separating Science Fiction From Fact By Carol Ann Brannon, MS, RD, LD, *Today's Dietitian*, Vol. 10 No. 4 P. 10

Okay, we've defined organic but what about those other labels? In the wise words of Harry Truman, "If you can't convince them, confuse them." Brother, it is confusing. Here are some terms you might see and what they mean.

- **Farm Fresh:** Tricky. If a corporate farm uses a robot to pick eggs from a hen, they can say "farm fresh" because it comes from a farm. Insulting to real farmers.
- **Certified Organic:** You already know this is bogus if it doesn't have the official USDA seal.
- **Premium Organic:** This is weird. It's not an official label. Maybe it just means you pay a premium price.
- **Made With Organic Ingredients:** The product must contain at least 70% organic ingredients. The remaining 30% of ingredients can be non-organic allowed ingredients or non-organic agricultural ingredients.
- **Fair Trade:** This means that the farmers and workers are paid fair prices and wages, work in safe conditions that also protect the environment.
- **Natural or Made From Natural Ingredients:** This has got to be one of the worst offenders. 'Natural" is not a regulated term. It means nothing. All ingredients are natural at some point in time.

GORDON SAYS: *Remember, organic ingredients must be grown without the use of pesticides, synthetic fertilizers, sewage sludge, genetically modified organisms or ionizing radiation.*

What's the deal with organic beer? Some guys think it's just for sissies. So wrong. So why should you drink it? First of all the barley, hops, and other ingredients used to make your fermented libation aren't subjected to toxic insecticides, herbicides, fungicides and fertilizers. Chemical free beer has no food additives or artificial flavoring. These hops are real. I'm not going to try to change your brand but it's worth a taste if you see it somewhere.

SUGAR—LOVE IT—LEAVE IT!

Sugar, by any other name, is still sugar and organic doesn't mean it won't contribute to weight gain or health problems. It also doesn't mean low calorie. What counts most is your sweetener's Glycemic Index (GI). This scale indicates how fast and how high a particular food can raise our blood glucose. Glucose runs every cell in your body and is the main source of energy for the brain. Ever wonder why you feel lightheaded when you work too hard and don't eat? It's hypoglycemia from low blood sugar (too little glucose). Glucose reacts with insulin; too much of it causes diabetes. An awareness of a food's GI can help you control your blood sugar levels, prevent heart disease, improve cholesterol, prevent certain cancers and achieve or maintain a healthy weight. Sugar and starchy foods are broken down by our bodies and converted to glucose. Excess glucose converts to fat and is stored in the body. Some foods, like white rice, enriched pasta, breads and sweets, convert to glucose quicker than others. Pure glucose has a GI of 100. High GI foods rank over 60, moderate, between 45 and 60, and low GI foods are below 45. Check out these lists of foods and their Glycemic Index. www.glycemicindex.ca/glycemicindexfoods.pdf[2]

---

2. *The Glucose Revolution* by J Brand-Miller PhD, T.M.S.Wolever MD, PhD, S Colagiuri MD, K Foster-Powell Mnutr.&Diet

THE CONFUSING WORLD OF SWEETENERS

- **Sucrose**, white table sugar, is half glucose and half fructose and is refined from sugar cane or sugar beets. Sucrose is a major element in confectionary and desserts because the fructose component has almost double the sweetness of glucose. The Glycemic Index (GI) of sucrose is 61, not much more than processed honey which has a GI of 55. You may see "extra fine" or "fine" because small crystals are not susceptible to caking.

- **Fructose** comes from fruit so is it better for you? Yes and no. It has a relatively low GI at 19 but consuming too much overwhelms the body's capacity to process it. Fructose is metabolized very differently in your body than glucose; all of the burden falls on your liver, in much the same way as alcohol, and fills your body with toxic by-products. There's also a big difference between fructose in fruit–where it's paired with fiber which slows down its absorption –and fructose that's refined into high fructose corn syrup.

- **High fructose corn syrup** is a manmade sweetener found in thousands of processed foods from ketchup to crackers and it definitely is not organic. The syrup was first introduced as a cheaper substitute to table sugar and sweetens just about all of the soda Americans drink. It is the number one source of calories in America. A can of soda contains around nine teaspoons of sugar in the form of high fructose corn syrup. This corn-based sugar replacement is a contributing factor to obesity in America, heart disease and diabetes[3]. A lot of people then jumped on the agave bandwagon, a natural, organic and a healthy alternative to sugar.

---

3. www.ajc.com/news/lifestyles/health/high-fructose-corn-syrup-linked-diabetes/nTG9x/

- **Agave** is the plant your tequila comes from, but for thousands of years it's been used as a sweetener. The nectar is known in Mexico as aguamiel, or "honey water." The Aztecs prized the agave as a gift from the gods. It's becoming the preferred sweetener of health conscious consumers and natural foods cooks alike. Wholesome® Blue Agave has a GI of 6.24, the lowest of the most popular brands.
- **Stevia**, another organic alternative, is an herb native to Paraguay and has been used as a natural sweetener and flavor enhancer for centuries. It has no calories and none of the unhealthy sugar drawbacks. Why? Because it as a glycemic index of zero! Try it...you might like it.
- **Dextrose** is a sweetener usually made from corn but can come from rice or other plant starch. Dextrose is altered chemically with enzymes and goes almost directly into the blood stream with a glycemic index of 100! Dextrose extends the shelf life of foods and helps to keep prepared foods from losing their color. Not organic!
- **Turbinado Sugar**, sometimes called Raw Sugar is created by spinning the moisture out of pure sugar cane. The result is a crunchy, coarse grained sugar that is golden in appearance due to the molasses that has remained. As an unrefined sugar, Turbinado sugar retains more of its nutrients than a refined sugar, and this variety is also certified organic. It's considered healthier because it's minimally refined.
- **Coconut Sugar**, the latest fad, is produced from the sap of cut flower buds of the coconut palm. It's been used as a traditional sweetener for thousands of years in the South and South-East Asian regions where the coconut palm is in abundant supply. The GI is a low 35.
- **Honey** is a natural sweetener that can increase energy, endurance and help reduce muscle fatigue. The glucose in honey is absorbed by the body quickly. This gives you an immediate energy boost; fructose, absorbed more slowly, provides sustained energy. Honey also keeps levels of blood

sugar fairly constant compared to other types of sugar. Try it before you work out. When you have that afternoon slow down at work, reach for the honey jar instead of soda, coffee or energy "shot."

GORDON SAYS: *Beware of cute little bear-shaped bottles or any other products that say "honey" but may not contain any pollen, which means they are processed and are not bona fide honey.*

- **Xylitol** sounds like a chemical but it's 100% natural. The white crystalline substance looks and tastes like sugar but is considered a "sugar free" sweetener and has a GI of 0. Also called sugar alcohol, it's found in berries, fruit, vegetables and mushrooms and occurs naturally in our bodies. An average size adult manufactures up to 15 grams of xylitol daily during normal metabolism. Check the product label because some products contain ingredients, fillers or other sweeteners that are not natural. Among its many claims are prevention of cavities.

- **Artificial sweeteners**, also called sugar substitutes like aspartame in (Nutra Sweet®, Equal®), saccharine (Sweet and Low®) and sucralose (Splenda®) are not only used in beverages, you can also find them listed in baked goods, frozen desserts and mixes, fruit preparations, chewing gums, candies, jam, juice, jellies, couch drops, breath mints, salad dressings and more. Lots of articles and studies report that they are toxic and may contribute to cancer.

People think these sweeteners can help them lose weight, but they can do the opposite. How? Well, basically, they separate sweet taste from calories. The taste buds tell the brain that food is coming in, but the body doesn't get the energy it's expecting. In tests with lab rats at Purdue University, this undermined the ability of the brain to judge how much was consumed, and, over time, they begin to overeat and gain weight. This finding may explain why increasing numbers of people in the United States lack the natural ability to regulate food intake and body weight.[4] The rats didn't have a choice but you do and I say go for the high fructose corn syrup over chemical sweeteners. Now, that's really asking you to "choose your poison."

"Let thy Food be thy Medicine and thy Medicine be thy Food."

—Hippocrates, Greek physician, father of modern medicine

FOOD MATTERS

We mentioned before that you are what you eat but what you eat could also cure what ails you. It's not so far out and here's a small example.

Before the 18th century, scurvy was rampant. This debilitating disease affected the muscles, limiting long-distance sea travel, often killing large numbers of passengers and crew. In 1740, citrus juice, usually lemon or lime, was added to the traditional daily ration of watered-down grog given to Admiral Edward Vernon's sailors. They were the healthiest men in the British navy but it wasn't until 1747 that Dr. James Lind formally conducted a clinical trial to find out why. He proved that it was the vitamin C in citrus which treated and even prevented the disease. Today, there is medical research that shows vitamins and minerals can help alleviate illness. Why isn't it widely publicized? There's no money it. The pharmaceutical corporations spend millions on researching drugs not cures. Do you think "Big Pharma" would tell you that Vitamin C could treat scurvy or would they prescribe an expensive pill instead? A lemon is just too cheap and doesn't make a profit for them. They haven't yet seen the benefit of investing in wellness. I won't go into it all here. I recommend that you watch the very enlightening film, *Food Matters*. This documentary exposes the trillion dollar, worldwide *sickness industry* and gives some scientifically verifiable solutions for overcoming illness naturally. Get it from Netflix or buy a copy at their website www. foodmatters.tv/shop/films-and-books.

This is a great site with a ton of information including a section on superfoods which are found in nature. They are superior sources of anti-oxidants and es-

---
4. www.purdue.edu/uns/html4ever/2004/040629.Swithers.research.html

sential nutrients we need but can't make ourselves. Superfoods pack a lot of punch for their weight and their price. Here are some of the top-rated ones.

- **Fruits and Berries**: They pack an incredible amount of nutritional goodness into a small package and can help control blood sugar. Raisins, cherries, blueberries, strawberries, blackberries, prunes, plums and oranges are high in anti-oxidants that fight free radicals, molecules responsible for aging and tissue damage. Blueberries lead the pack. Kiwis are among the most nutritionally dense fruits. One large kiwi supplies the daily requirement for vitamin C.
- **Nuts**: Pistachios, almonds, peanuts, walnuts, cashews, and pecans are high in protein, heart-healthy fats, high fiber and antioxidants. Almonds have the highest concentration of overall nutrients per calorie and per ounce. Don't overindulge because nuts can pack on the pounds. An ounce a day will help fill you up. Add them to salads, cereals or entrees.
- **Whole Grains**: Barley, oats, buckwheat, whole wheat, wild rice and millet are good sources of soluble fiber which helps lower cholesterol. Start the day off with oatmeal, but not the instant sugary kind. I like quick-cooking, steel-cut oats topped with agave or pure maple syrup. Use rolled oats in a meatloaf instead of breadcrumbs. Quinoa, an ancient grain prepared like rice, is rich in zinc, vitamin E and selenium. It helps to control weight and lower the risk of heart disease and diabetes.
- **Beans**: They're loaded with insoluble fiber that helps to fill you up and also prevent constipation. Beans are low in fat and a good source of magnesium and potassium, nutrients that work together to lower blood pressure. If you're not cooking them from scratch, choose the canned ones without salt.
- **Yogurt**: What makes yogurt a superfood is the presence of prebiotics and probiotics. These living organisms promote gastrointestinal health and enhance immune function. The "good" bacteria found in yogurt can

help replace the beneficial intestinal flora antibiotics kill, enhances digestion, increases mineral absorption and synthesizes certain B vitamins. Yogurt is high in calcium. One cup of yogurt has 450 milligrams, compared to 300 milligrams in a cup of milk.

- **Greens**: Spinach, kale, watercress, parsley, lettuce, endive, chicory, broccoli, dandelion greens and sprouts contain high doses of chlorophyll, easily digestible proteins, enzymes and a wide range of vitamins and minerals. Raw leafy greens act as mini-transfusions for the blood, a health tonic for the brain and immune system and a cleanser of the kidneys.
- **Green Foods**: Wild blue green algae contains virtually every nutrient and can improve brain function. Wheat grass is super alkalizing, promotes healthy blood and normalizes the thyroid gland to stimulate metabolism. Chlorella is a fresh water algae that helps prevent hardening of the arteries. Spirulina contains 70% complete protein. It controls blood sugar levels and cravings making it a good food for diabetics, weight loss and as a general nutritional supplement. You can get green foods in powdered form, alone or in combination, as a great addition to your morning smoothie.
- **Eggs**: They make the list because eggs contain 12 vitamins and minerals, including choline which is good for brain development and memory. Among protein foods, eggs contain the richest mix of essential amino acids. The high levels of antioxidants found in eggs could even help prevent age-related macular degeneration - a leading cause of blindness. Eggs got a bad rap around cholesterol but research has shown that healthy adults can eat eggs without significantly impacting the risk of heart disease.

I hope you see the bottom line now. Food matters…to your health, to your state of mind, to your longevity. One small step for you, one giant leap toward your total wellness.

FOOD RULES

One of my heroes is Michael Pollan who has been a food crusader for years. His revolutionary book, *Omnivore's Dilemma: A Natural History of Four Meals* deals with the question that's confronted man since the cave and is still a number one issue….what to have for dinner! Pollan says everything he's learned about food and health can be summed up in seven words: "Eat food, not too much, mostly plants." He means real food -- vegetables, fruits, whole grains, and, yes, fish and meat. Pollan warns us to avoid "edible food-like substances." I think cheese in a can is a prime example. He also points out that overall, American eating habits have contributed to the high cost of health care. Over three quarters of the two-trillion that we spend goes to treat chronic diseases; many of these can be prevented by a change in lifestyle, especially diet. Pollan's book, *Food Rules* is a great guide to saving males and everyone else on the planet. It's a very funny, quick read. Here are a few of my favorites:

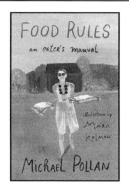

"If it came from a plant, eat it; if it was made in a plant, don't.

Don't eat breakfast cereals that change the color of the milk.

Don't eat anything with more than five ingredients, or ingredients you can't pronounce.

Don't eat anything your great grandmother wouldn't recognize as food.

Don't buy food where you buy your gasoline.

Eat all the junk food you want as long as you cook it yourself."

And that's where I come in. I'm not a food Nazi or a fanatic who tells you to ditch dessert or completely cut carbs. I'm just saying there are ways you can eat that won't wreck your health. Guys, you're worth saving, not for your friends, your family or anyone else…you're worth saving for you.

NOTES:

Chef Gordon Smith has over 25 years combined experience both as a chef and company owner. A California native, he trained under legendary chefs including Michel Stroot of the Golden Door and became a respected specialist in spa cuisine. Chef Gordon was instrumental in opening Deepak Chopra's Center for Well Being in La Jolla. Later, he served as executive chef for major resorts in California. During the Los Angeles Olympics, he worked as kitchen manager feeding the athletes in addition to catering presidential and mayoral events. He was a member of the American Natural Food Team which won two silver medals at the Culinary Olympics in Germany. Chef Gordon was twice awarded Best Chef of North County for his own restaurant, Basil Street Café in Encinitas, where he also owned a full service catering business. His interest in preserving the small farmer led him to found Slow Food San Diego. He served a four year term as Governor of Slow Food Southern California and was selected as a delegate to the Slow Food Terra Madre, an international food conference of 150 countries. His past private chef clients include First Lady Betty Ford, Michael Eisner, Saudi Prince Fahad and James Garner among many others. In addition to his mission to save the males, Chef Gordon serves on the advisory board of Home Town Farms which specializes in vertical growing. He is currently president of the board of The Encinitas Community Garden.

Brooklyn-born, **Reparata Mazzola** is a published author and produced screenwriter. She was a contributing editor for several magazines, is a member of the Writers Guild of America and served on its Board of Directors. Before launching her full-time writing career, Reparata was an Emmy-nominated television producer in New York but left her TV career to sing, recording and touring the world as a member of Barry Manilow's backup trio, Lady Flash. Relocation to Los Angeles led to acting. Her own production company co-produced a movie she wrote and starred in. Reparata authored a best-selling biography, also penning the screenplay which is being produced as a feature film. Reparata lives in Los Angeles with a chef, a cat and a variety of friendly wildlife. Her meatballs are legendary.

WEBLIOGRAPHY

The URL addresses are accurate as of this printing. If any link doesn't work, just search the subject and you'll get updated information.

RECOMMENDED RECIPE SITES

allrecipes.com — Includes really easy ones with just 5 ingredients, videos, and a convertor in each recipe that scales portion sizes.

GORDON SAYS: *These sites are great for beginners and even advanced cooks. Remember to put "easy" or "simple" in your search. They also have a wide selection of healthy and, except for the beef site, lots of vegetarian recipes.*

delish.com — Recipes listed by ease and cuisine, special occasions and the site has a serving size convertor.

food.com — Great for all cuisines. Includes tips and an online weekly meal planner.

cookinglight.com — Focus is on weight, healthy recipes and party fare.

jamieoliver.com — British chef Jamie started the "Food Revolution" to stop obesity, especially in children. With a focus on cooking, his website has recipes, meal planning, restaurants, videos from his show and more. This is a one-stop shop.

BeefItsWhatsForDinner.com — Where's the beef? Right here…all you need to know for you and some recipes for kids too.

kidshealth.org/kid/recipes — This site not only has recipes, it also features some for kids with health issues such as diabetes and celiac. A bonus is that all the recipes are recorded so you and the kids can follow them together.

cakeshapesdesigns.com — Has inexpensive downloadable cake patterns with easy step-by-step instructions. No fancy shaped pans or decorating skills are required. Fun for both kids' and adults' cakes.

GORDON'S TIP: *If you have your own recipe, this site will convert the serving sizes for you.* **free-online-calculator-use.com/recipe-conversion-calculator.html#calculator** *If you don't have an ingredient in the house and want to make the recipe, here's a list of common substitutions.* **allrecipes.com/howto/common-ingredient-substitutions**

OTHER COOL SITES:

FIND A FARMERS' MARKET NEAR YOU

Support your area farmer and reduce the carbon footprint by buying local.

www.ams.usda.gov/farmersmarkets/index.htm

FIND A CSA

Community Supported Agriculture is a food co-op where a local farmer grows food and delivers it to the member/shareholders. **www.nal.usda.gov/afsic/csa**

BODY MASS INDEX CALCULATOR

An indicator of body fat calculated from your weight and height.

www.healthcalculators.org/calculators/bmi.asp

BASAL METABOLISM CALCULATOR

Measures the number calories you need to maintain normal body functions. The higher the BMR, the faster you burn calories.

www.calculator.net/bmr-calculator.html

CALORIE/ACTIVITY CALCULATOR

This will tell you the recommended number of calories per day for your activity level. **www.freedieting.com/tools/calorie_calculator.htm**

FAT INTAKE CALCULATOR

Find the right amount of fat recommended for your diet.

www.healthcalculators.org/calculators/fat.asp

GYLCEMIC INDEX CALCULATOR

This scale indicates how fast and how high a particular food can raise your blood glucose. Glucose runs every cell in your body and is the main source of energy for the brain. **www.glycemicindex.ca/glycemicindexfoods.pdf**

NUTRITION DATA

nutritiondata.com — From *Self* magazine, this is a comprehensive site with lots of valuable information. You can even calculate the nutrition of your own recipes. The nutrition management tools are bonus including an online tracker for weight loss, a heart health section and a unit convertor, among many others.

FAST FOOD NUTRITION INFO

fastfoodnutrition.org — Nutrition facts for over 4,000 menu items from the most popular fast food restaurants.

BEANS

usdrybeans.com — Everything you want to know about this healthy, tasty, protein alternative: nutrition, bean varieties and recipes.

SUPER FOODS

foodmatters.tv — The real skinny on why superfoods are super and a great documentary on the subject.

ORGANIC MEAT

heritagefoodsusa.com — All animals that come from Heritage are anti-biotic free and raised on pasture.

CHIPS

beanfieldssnacks.com — These delicious snacks made from beans are non-GMO, gluten free, corn free, vegan and I will add…delicious.

ARTISAN BEER

stonebrewing.com — Stone Brewing Co. is a premiere, award-winning craft brewer and my beer of choice. Check the website for the latest brew and the "find" link to see where it's available in your area.

stoneworldbistro.com — These two unique restaurants feature a sustainable eclectic menu of world-inspired cuisine. In Escondido, a brewery tour is $3 and includes a guided Stone beer tasting. Forbes ranked it as "America's Best Brewery Tour."

EDIBLE SCHOOLYARD

edibleschoolyard.org — The Edible Schoolyard Project builds gardens as interactive classrooms to transform the food values and health of children and teens. The movement was started by Alice Waters, Berkley Chef who founded Chez Panisse, the pioneer restaurant known for using local, organic foods. She is credited as the inspiration for the California cuisine style of cooking.

BOOKS I DIDN'T WRITE BUT RECOMMEND!

The Magic of Fire: Hearth Cooking: One Hundred Recipes for the Fireplace or Campfire by William Rubel
This is one of my favorite cookbooks. It takes outdoor cuisine to another level exploring both the techniques of hearth cooking and its tradition through the ages.

The New Basics Cookbook by Shelia Lukins and Julee Rosso
One of my go-to reference cookbooks. It's filled with cooking tips, menus, kitchen wisdom, quotes and food lore. Recipes include interesting ingredients from around the world.

Mexico — One Plate at a Time by Rick Bayless
If you have one Mexican cookbook, this is it. It's the companion to the PBS television series of the same name and is user friendly.

Molto Gusto: Easy Italian Cooking by Mario Bitali
This is a great pizza-making book for the amateur or advanced cook. Bitali also includes a collection of recipes for Italian favorites from pasta and antipasto to gelato.

Vegetarian Cooking for Everyone by Debra Madison
A comprehensive soup-to-nuts book for anyone who wants to eat more vegetables. You don't have to be a vegetarian but it's a great book for that lifestyle and for vegans too.

Meals in 30 Minutes by Jamie Oliver
After a hard day at work, Chef Jamie shows that you can make a whole quick meal without compromising quality. I like his food philosophy and like the recipes in his book.

What Einstein Told His Cook: Kitchen Science Explained by Robert Wolke
Never thought I'd find a science book fascinating. These witty explanations to common food questions in plain, non-technical language make science fun.

Food Rules and Cooked by Michael Pollan
One of my foodie heroes, Michael Pollan has reached the masses to promote the

idea that "you are what you cook" and other worthwhile philosophy. All of his books are worth reading.

Eggs by Michel Roux — Each chapter is based around a style of cooking eggs, from boiling, frying ,poaching, baking and scrambling, to making the perfect omelet, crêpe, soufflé, meringue and custard. Gives Includes classic sauces, like Hollandaise, with a light, modern twist.

How to Repair Food by John and Marina Bear — A comprehensive guide that helps you fix things when you goof up in the kitchen.

Opps by Cooking Light — This book has 209 solutions for everyday kitchen mistakes.

AND FINALLY…

slowfoodusa.com — Slow Food preserves cultural food traditions. They also defend and advocate policies that promote holistic alternatives to the industrial system. I like their focus on return to the table as a center of pleasure for family and friends. The movement started in Europe and is now in 150 countries.

hometownfarms.com — Their mission is to provide high quality, locally-grown organic food to the people in urban communities where space and soil are at a premium. Vertical growing saves natural resources, eliminates waste and is the future of farming. Search: "vertical growing systems" to find a system that suits your space. The one in the book that I have in my house comes from vertigro.com

slowmoney.com — The Slow Money Alliance brings people together around a new conversation about finance that is disconnected from people and place and about how we can begin fixing our economy from the ground up... starting with food.

farmaid.org — This nonprofit organization helps keep family farmers on their land to keep growing good food for us all. Willie Nelson, Neil Young, John Mellencamp and Dave Matthews organized the first benefit concert.

APPENDIX

Conversion Table

UNIT	DRY MEASURE	LIQUID MEASURE
1 teaspoon	1/3 tablespoon	1/6 fluid ounce
1 tablespoon	3 teaspoons	1/2 fluid ounce
2 tablespoons	1/8 cup (6 teaspoons)	1 fluid ounce
4 tablespoons	1/4 cup (12 teaspoons)	2 fluid ounces
1/8 cup	2 tablespoons	1 fluid ounce
1/4 cup	4 tablespoons	2 fluid ounces
1/3 cup	5 tablespoons + 1 teaspoon	2- 2/3 fluid ounces
1/2 cup	8 tablespoons	4 fluid ounces
2/3 cup	10 tablespoons + 2 teaspoons	5-1/3 fluid ounces
3/4 cup	12 tablespoons	6 fluid ounces
7/8 cup	14 tablespoons	7 fluid ounces
1 cup	16 tablespoons	8 fluid ounces / 1/2 pint
2 cups	32 tablespoons	16 fluid ounces / 1 pint
4 cups	1 quart	32 fluid ounces
1 pint	32 tablespoons	16 fluid ounces / 1 pint
2 pints	1.0 quart	32 fluid ounces
8 pints	4 quarts	1 gallon/ 128 fluid ounces

Here's a free online site that will convert the most common kitchen measurements and some other useful cooking conversions. **www.onlineconversion.com/cooking.htm**

- Weight to Volume: Convert grams to cups and more
- Butter: Convert between sticks of butter and grams, cups, tablespoons, etc.
- Oven Temperature: Convert between gas and electric temperatures.

In addition to cooking, there are great calculators for things you also might want to convert, including metric.

Recipe Terms:

- Tbs or Tbsp = tablespoon
- Tsp = teaspoon
- Oz = ounce
- C = cup
- Season to taste: You can add as much or as little as you want.
- Dash/Pinch = around 1/16th teaspoon'.
- Mince: Chop into tiny pieces.
- Beat: Briskly stir with a spoon, fork or electric mixture.
- Grease: Coat with a thin coat of oil, butter or cooking spray.
- Blend: Mix together so you can't see the separate ingredients.
- Sear: Cooking meat with high heat for a short time to seal in juices.
- Baste: Spoon liquid over meat during cooking to avoid drying out.

100 grams equals...

- (1/5 pound or 3.5 ounces)
- 1 stick of butter, or a little less than half a cup
- 1/2 a medium sized apple
- 2 fried eggs
- 1 medium sized banana
- 3/4 cup of all purpose flour
- 1/2 cup of cooked rice
- 5 slices of commercial white bread
- 1/2 of a medium sized baked potato
- 1/4 pound of t-bone steak
- 50 teaspoons of dried oregano
- 1/4 pound of tuna steak
- 1 medium sized tomato
- 1/3 of a 16oz can of beer (or soft drink)
- 1/2 a cup of cooked ground beef, 25 grams per ounce to make a 1/4 pound.

STORAGE GUIDELINES

U.S. Food & Drug Administration Center for Food Safety and Nutrition
www.fda.gov

Fruit Storage

FRESH FRUIT	REFRIGERATOR	FREEZER
Apples	1 month	8-12 months
Apricots, grapes, nectarines	3-5 days	8-12 months
Avocados	3-5 days	8-12 months
Bananas, plantains	Not recommended	8-12 months
Berries, cherries	2-3 days	8-12 months
Grapefruit, lemons, limes, oranges	2 weeks	4-6 months
Guavas, papayas	1-2 days	8-12 months
Kiwis	3-5 days	4-6 months
Melons	1 week	8-12 months
Peaches, pears, plums	3-5 days	8-12 months
Pineapple	2-3 days	4-6 months

Seasonal Produce

	FRUITS	VEGGIES
Summer	berries, cherries, apricots, peaches, melons, plums, mangoes, grapes, tomatoes, eggplant	green beans, sweet corn, peppers, zucchini
Fall	apples, pumpkins, pears, persimmons	cauliflower, yams, broccoli, collards, Brussels sprouts
Winter	oranges, grapefruit, avocadoes	carrots, onions, acorn squash, turnips, cabbage, sweet potatoes
Spring	blackberries, strawberries, cucumbers	asparagus, lettuce, spinach, red radish, green onions, new potatoes

Vegetable Storage

VEGETABLE	REFRIGERATOR	FREEZER (Blanched)
Artichokes	1 week	Not recommended
Asparagus	2-3 days	8-12 months
Beets, carrots	2 weeks	8-12 months
Beans, broccoli, peas	3-5 days	8-12 months
Cauliflower	1 week	8-12 months
Corn (husk on)	3-5 days	8-12 months
Green onions	3-5 days	Not recommended
Celery, cabbage, chilies, green beans	1 week	8-12 months
Green beans, tomatoes	1 week	8-12 months
Greens: collard, spinach, Swiss chard	3-5 days	8-12 months (blanched)
Lettuce and salad greens	1 week	Not recommended
Mushrooms	1-2 days	8-12 months (blanched)
Radishes	2 weeks	Not recommended
Small Summer squash	1-2 days	8-12 months
Large Winter squash (pumpkins)	Not recommended	Not recommended

Cheese

Melting		Non-Melting
Asiago	Gruyere	Fresh Mexican cheeses:
Bel Paese	Havarti	Queso Blanco, Queso Fresco
Brie	Jarlsberg	Ranchero, Cotija
Cheddar	Monterey Jack	Indian Paneer
Colby	Mozzarella	Cottage cheese
Edam	Muenster	Ricotta (except when baking it)
Fontina	Provolone	Goat cheese
Gouda	Swiss	Feta

Guide to Safely Refreezing Thawed Food
www.agriculture.ny.gov/FS/consumer/thawed.html

FROZEN UNCOOKED	THAWED - COLD (45° or lower)	THAWED - WARM (above 45°)
Fruit	Yes	Probably safe - but may have fermented
Fruit Juice Concentrate	Yes, but flavor may be poor and reconstituted juice separates	No - may have fermented
Vegetables	Yes	Questionable - safer not to refreeze - especially corn, peas, and beans - discard
Meat	Yes, if odor is normal. If any odor, discard	Do not refreeze
Poultry	Yes - if odor is normal - If there is any odor - discard	No
Fish and Shellfish	Yes, if odor is normal. If there is any off odor, discard	No
Cooked Meat, Poultry and Fish	No	No
Combination Dishes, Pot Pies, Casseroles, Whole Meals	No	No
Soups	No	No
Ice Cream and Sherbet	No	No
Fruit Pies	Yes	Yes - but quality may be poor
Plain Cake and Cookies	Yes	Yes - but texture may be poor
Cream-filled Cake and Cookies	No	No

Refrigerator and Freezer Storage Chart

www.fda.gov/downloads/Food/ResourcesForYou/HealthEducators/UCM109315.pdf

FOOD ITEM	REFRIGERATOR	FREEZER
Eggs		
Fresh, in shell	4 to 5 weeks	Don't Freeze
Raw yolks, whites	2 to 4 days	1 year
Hard Boiled	1 week	Not recommended
Deli Products		
Mayonnaise, (refrigerate after opening)	2 months	Don't freeze
Egg, chicken, tuna, ham, macaroni salads	3 to 5 days	Not recommended
Meat (Beef, Veal, Lamb, & Pork)		
Stew meats	1 to 2 days	3 to 4 months
Ground turkey, veal, pork, lamb	1 to 2 days	3 to 4 months
Steaks	3 to 5 days	6 to 12 months
Chops	3 to 5 days	4 to 6 months
Roasts	3 to 5 days	4 to 12 months
Bacon	7 days	1 month
Sausage, pork, beef, chicken or turkey	1 to 2 days	1 to 2 months
Smoked breakfast links, patties	7 days	1 to 2 months
Hot dogs, opened package	1 week	1 to 2 months
Hot dogs, unopened package	2 weeks	1 to 2 months
Lunch meats, opened package	3 to 5 days	1 to 2 months
Lunch meats, unopened package	2 weeks	1 to 2 months
Corned beef in pouch with pickling juices	5 to 7 days	Drained, 1 month
Ham, fully cooked, whole	7 days	1 to 2 months
Ham, fully cooked, half	3 to 5 days	1 to 2 months
Ham, fully cooked, slices	3 to 4 days	1 to 2 months

FOOD ITEM	REFRIGERATOR	FREEZER
Meat Leftovers		
Cooked meat & meat dishes	3 to 4 days	2 to 3 months
Gravy & meat broth	1 to 2 days	2 to 3 months
Cooked meat & meat dishes	3 to 4 days	2 to 3 months
Soups & Stews		
Vegetable or meat-added & mixtures	3 to 4 days	2 to 3 months
Fresh Poultry		
Chicken or turkey, whole	1 to 2 days	1 year
Chicken or turkey, parts	1 to 2 days	9 months
Giblets	1 to 2 days	3 to 4 months
Cooked Poultry, Leftover		
Fried chicken	3 to 4 days	4 months
Cooked poultry dishes	3 to 4 days	4 to 6 months
Pieces, plain	3 to 4 days	4 months
Pieces covered with broth, gravy	1 to 2 days	6 months
Chicken nuggets, patties	1 to 2 days	1 to 3 months
Fish & Shellfish		
Lean fish	1 to 2 days	6 months
Fatty fish	1 to 2 days	2 to 3 months
Cooked fish	3 to 4 days	4 to 6 months
Smoked fish	14 days	2 months
Fresh shrimp, scallops, crawfish, squid	1 to 2 days	3 to 6 months
Canned seafood, Pantry, 5 years	after opening 3 to 4 days	out of can 2 months

Internal Cooking Temperatures (approximate)

MEAT	Internal Temperatures (approximate)
BEEF	
Boneless roast, tenderloin	Well done: 170°
POULTRY	
Whole chicken / turkey	180°
Poultry-breast	170°
Duck	180°
LAMB	
Leg of lamb, rack of lamb	Rare: 125° Medium Rare: 130° Medium: 140° Medium Well: 150° Well Done: 160°
GROUND MEAT LOAVES	
Beef, veal, pork, turkey, chicken	160°

Alcohol Burn-Off Chart

Preparation Method:	% Retained
Alcohol added to boiling liquid & removed from heat	85%
Alcohol flamed	75%
No heat, stored overnight	70%
Baked, 25 minutes, alcohol not stirred into mixture	45%
Baked/simmered dishes with alcohol stirred into mixture:	
15 minutes cooking time	40%
30 minutes cooking time	35%
1 hour cooking time	25%
1.5 hours cooking time	20%
2 hours cooking time	10%
2.5 hours cooking time	5%

Beer Calorie Chart

Brand	Calories	Carbs (g)	% Alcohol
Amstel Light	95	5	3.5
Budweiser	145	10.6	5
Bud Light	110	6.6	4.2
Coors	149	12.2	5
Coors Light	102	5	4.2
Corona	148	14	4.6
Corona Light	99	5	3.2
Guinness Stout	176	14	6
Guinness Draught	126	10	4
Heineken	148	11.3	5
Heineken Light	99	6.8	3.5
Miller Genuine Draft	143	13.1	4.7
Miller MGD 64	64	2.4	2.8
Sam Adams	180	18.8	4.9
Sam Adams Light	119	9.6	4
Stella Artois	154	11.6	5.2

Alcohol Calorie Chart

Drink	Calories
80 proof alcohol -1 oz	80
Wine - 5 oz. glass	100-110
Beer, 12 oz regular	145
Beer, light	105
Beer, lager	120
Beer, strong	180
Beer, stout	190
Scotch – 1 oz	65
Mai Tai – 4.5 oz	310
Pina Colada - 4.5 oz	300
Gin/Vodka Tonic- 4.5 oz	200
Gin/Vodka Diet Tonic	100
Bloody Mary - 5 oz	116
Martini- 3 oz gin or vodka	190
Margarita - 4 oz	248

Save The Males Cookbook

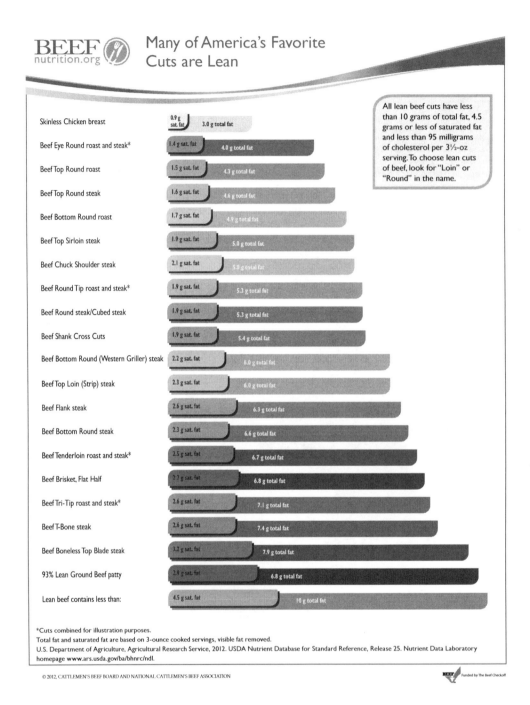

Courtesy of The Beef Checkoff www.BeefItsWhatsForDinner.com

Appendix

BEEF nutrition.org — Nutrient Bang for Your Calorie Buck

3-OUNCE COOKED SERVING	CALORIES	TOTAL FAT (g)	SFA (g)	MUFA (g)	CHOLESTEROL (mg)	PROTEIN (g)	IRON (mg)	ZINC (mg)	SELENIUM (mcg)	RIBOFLAVIN (mg)	NIACIN (mg)	B_6 (mg)	PHOSPHORUS (mg)	CHOLINE (mg)	B_{12} (mcg)
BEEF															
Daily Value*	2000	65	20	N/A	300	50	18	15	70	1.7	20	2	1,000	550**	6
Beef Eye Round roast & steak	144	4.0	1.4	1.7	65	25	2.1	4.3	28.3	0.14	4.5	0.3	158	96	1.4
Beef Top Round roast	169	4.3	1.5	1.6	76	31	2.8	3.9	28	0.21	3.2	0.2	192	117	2.3
Beef Top Round steak	157	4.6	1.6	1.9	71	27	2.3	4.7	30.9	0.15	4.9	0.4	173	103	1.5
Beef Bottom Round roast	139	4.9	1.7	2.0	65	24	2.0	4.1	26.9	0.13	4.3	0.3	150	91	1.3
Beef Top Sirloin steak	151	5.0	1.9	2.0	67	25	1.6	4.6	29.2	0.13	7.2	0.5	198	95	1.4
Beef Chuck Shoulder steak	149	5.0	2.1	2.6	70	24	2.5	7.0	27.2	0.19	4.7	0.6	212	75	2.9
Beef Round Tip roast & steak	148	5.3	1.9	2.2	63	23	2.0	4.0	26.4	0.13	4.2	0.3	148	89	1.3
Beef Round steak/ Cubed steak	154	5.3	1.9	2.3	66	25	2.3	4.0	23.5	0.19	3.6	0.3	218	95	2.7
Beef Shank Cross Cuts	171	5.4	1.9	2.4	66	29	3.3	8.9	25.5	0.18	5.0	0.3	224	N/A	3.2
Beef Bottom Round (Western Griller) steak	155	6.0	2.2	2.7	65	23	2.5	4.3	37.1	0.18	6.4	0.6	198	79	3.4
Beef Top Loin (Strip) steak	161	6.0	2.3	2.4	69	25	1.6	4.6	28.8	0.13	7.1	0.5	196	95	1.4
Beef Flank steak	158	6.3	2.6	2.5	66	24	1.5	4.3	27.1	0.12	6.8	0.5	184	90	1.4
Beef Bottom Round steak	184	6.6	2.3	2.7	80	29	2.4	5.0	33.0	0.17	5.2	0.4	185	111	1.6
Beef Tenderloin roast & steak	164	6.7	2.5	2.7	69	24	1.5	4.5	28	0.12	6.9	0.5	191	92	1.4
Beef Brisket, Flat Half	181	6.8	2.7	2.9	78	28	2.3	6.5	26.3	0.17	4.0	0.3	170	107	2.1
Beef Tri-Tip roast & steak	155	7.1	2.6	3.6	66	23	1.4	4.2	26.3	0.12	6.5	0.5	179	87	1.3
Beef T-Bone steak	161	7.4	2.6	3.5	47	22	3.1	4.3	8.5	0.21	3.9	0.3	183	84	1.9
Beef Boneless Top Blade steak	167	7.9	3.2	3.8	81	24	2.7	8.4	26.7	0.27	3.7	0.3	190	90	4.4
93% Lean Ground Beef patty	154	6.8	2.9	2.8	67	22	2.4	5.4	17.8	0.15	5.2	0.3	187	71	2.6
PORK															
Daily Value*	2000	65	20	N/A	300	50	18	15	70	1.7	20	2	1,000	550**	6
Top Loin chop	147	5.2	1.8	2.3	61	23	0.5	1.8	38.5	0.17	7.2	0.6	201	67	0.5
Tenderloin	122	3.0	1.0	1.1	62	22	1.0	2.1	32.5	0.33	6.3	0.6	227	76	0.5
Sirloin chop	166	5.9	2.0	2.4	75	26	0.6	1.8	40.3	0.23	6.8	0.5	258	76	0.5
Rib chop	158	7.1	2.4	3.0	56	22	0.6	1.9	38.6	0.19	6.7	0.6	185	62	0.4
POULTRY															
Daily Value*	2000	65	20	N/A	300	50	18	15	70	1.7	20	2	1,000	550**	6
Skinless, Boneless Chicken breast	140	3.0	0.9	1.1	72	26	0.9	0.9	23.5	0.1	11.7	0.5	194	73	0.3
Skinless, Boneless Turkey breast	115	0.6	0.2	0.1	71	26	1.3	1.5	27.3	0.11	6.4	0.5	190	72	0.3
FISH															
Daily Value*	2000	65	20	N/A	300	50	18	15	70	1.7	20	2	1,000	550**	6
Cod	89	0.7	0.1	0.1	47	19	0.4	0.5	32	0.07	2.1	0.2	117	71	0.9
Light Tuna Canned in Water	99	0.7	0.2	0.1	26	22	1.3	0.7	68.3	0.06	11.3	0.3	139	25	2.5
Halibut	94	1.4	0.3	0.5	51	19	0.2	0.4	47.1	0.03	6.7	0.5	244	64	1.1
Salmon	130	4.5	0.8	1.4	47	21	0.4	0.4	32	0.11	8.2	0.6	266	96	4

*Daily Value based on a 2000-calorie intake for adults and children 4 or more years of age. Source: USDA. · ** 550mg is the highest adequate intake (AI) for choline.

© 2012, CATTLEMEN'S BEEF BOARD AND NATIONAL CATTLEMEN'S BEEF ASSOCIATION   18314   Funded by The Beef Checkoff

Courtesy of The Beef Checkoff www.BeefItsWhatsForDinner.com

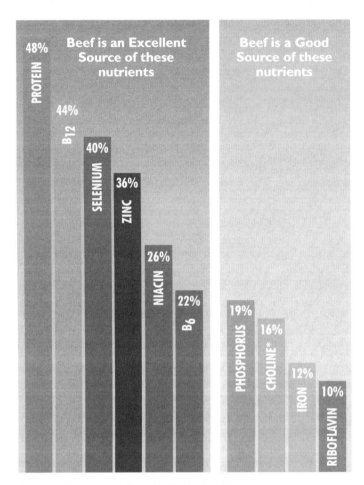

Courtesy of The Beef Checkoff www.BeefItsWhatsForDinner.com

INDEX

A

Appetizers
- Guacamole 135
- Macho Nachos 140
- Mushroom & Walnut Paté 88
- My Tortilla Chips 141
- Quick Black Bean Dip 138
- Sensational Seven Layer Bean Dip 137
- Shrimp Mousse on Cucumber Rounds 89
- Wondrous White Bean Dip 138

B

Basic Cooking Techniques 37

C

Chicken
- Chicken Marsala 126
- Cornish Hens with Apricot Glaze 90
- Gordon's Wings 139
- In-the-Bag Chicken & Vegetables 125
- Leftover Chicken and Rice 50
- Orange Chicken 91

E

Essential Utensils 20

F

Fish
- Fish Tacos 117
- Poached Salmon in Dill Sauce 93
- Sensational Salmon Broil 124
- Tips for Baking Salmon 123
- Tuna Pattie Sliders 167

Food Storage 33

K

Kids
- Amazing Ambrosia 170
- Breakfast Pita Pockets 159
- Cheesy Chimichangas 166
- Chicken Fingers 168
- Easy Tortilla Pizza 157
- Fool Proof Parfait 170
- Gordon's Hamburgers 164
- Morning Egg Pizzas 162
- Nacho Casserole 164
- No Bake Cake 169
- Peanut Butter Stuffed French Toast 161
- Scratch Pancakes 159
- Simple Sloppy Joe's 165
- South of the Border Pizza 158
- The Perfect Hard Boiled Egg 162
- Tortilla Chip Scramble 163
- Tuna Pattie Sliders 167

M

Meat
- Game Day Deli Sliders 142
- Gordon's Hamburgers 164
- Lean Beef & Broccoli Stir Fry 114
- Leftover Meatloaf Parmigiana 75
- Meatloaf Variations 74
- Mouth Watering Meatloaf 74
- Oven Barbequed Beef Short Ribs 95
- Oven Cooked Steaks 72
- Sherry-Apple Pork Chops 94
- Slow Roasted Pork Loin 113
- Terrific Turkey Chili 136

P

Pasta/Sauces
- Basic Marinara Sauce 56
- Basic Pesto Sauce 59
- Chef Gordon's Sauce 144
- Garlic & Oil Sauce (Al Olio) 60
- Good for You Macaroni and Cheese 129
- Marinara Sauce Variations 57
- Pasta Primavera 92
- Pasta with Broccoli 62
- Quick Classic Alfredo Sauce 60
- Reparata's Brooklyn Meat Sauce 58
- Sweet Pepper Sauce 61
- Tantalizing Tofu Lasagna 130
- Teriyaki Marinade 139

R

Rice
  Basic Rice Pilaf 48
  Fried Rice, Twice As Nice 50
  Leftover Chicken & Rice 50
  Nice and Easy Rice 48
  Simple Spanish Rice 51

Romance
  Cheesy Ham & Egg Crescents 100
  Chocolate Dipped Strawberries 97
  Fruit Cobbler 98
  Perfect Peach Bellini 101
  Sexy Scramble 100
  Simple Caesar Salad 96
  Strawberry Kissed French Toast 98
  Strawberry Kisses 99
  Sweet Morning Quiche 99

S

Smoothies
  Breakfast Smoothie 121
  Gordon's Hangover Smoothie 151

Stocking Your Pantry 25

V

Vegetables
  Garlic Mashed Potatoes 69
  How to Peel and Seed Tomatoes 57
  Make Ahead Potato Skins 69
  Manly Mashed Potatoes 68
  Potatoes: Baked 66
  Potatoes: Boiled, Steamed 65
  Pounds Off Soup 128
  Roasted Peppers 61
  Steamed Veggie Mania 122
  Tantalizing Tofu Lasagna 130
  Tempting Tempeh with Peanut Sauce 131